COURAGEOUS GRANDPARENTING

REVISED

Building a Legacy Worth Outliving You

Revised and Updated for a
New Generation of Grandparents

Published by
The Christian Grandparenting Network
Colorado Springs, CO

CAVIN HARPER

COURAGEOUS GRANDPARENTING

When all is said and done, it is my prayer and earnest desire that what is written in these pages can only be expressed thus: Soli Deo Gloria!

What People are Saying About *Courageous Grandparenting*

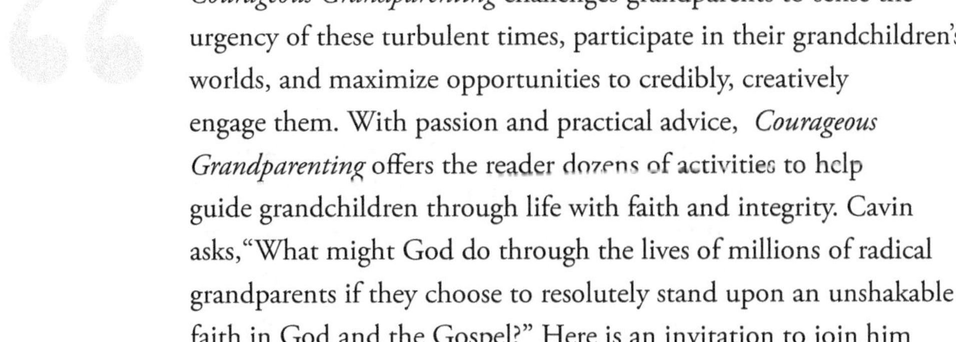

Cavin Harper is every grandparent's "new best friend!" *Courageous Grandparenting* is filled with all the right stuff—stories and statistics, ideas and ideals, humor and hopefulness. He lays out the power of words and blessings and shows us how we can offer them up as sacred gifts. With a strong reminder that "we're not in Kansas anymore," he helps us share values and virtues with the ones who want to hear from the gray champions in their lives. Thanks, Cavin, for a timely epistle and a great read!"

—DR. WARD TANNEBERG, President/Executive Director, The CASA Network

Courageous Grandparenting challenges grandparents to sense the urgency of these turbulent times, participate in their grandchildren's worlds, and maximize opportunities to credibly, creatively engage them. With passion and practical advice, *Courageous Grandparenting* offers the reader dozens of activities to help guide grandchildren through life with faith and integrity. Cavin asks, "What might God do through the lives of millions of radical grandparents if they choose to resolutely stand upon an unshakable faith in God and the Gospel?" Here is an invitation to join him and other grandparents who share a passion to invest their lives in radical grandparenting for such a time as this."

—LINDA THOMAS, Author: Grandma's Letters from Africa
www.grandmaslettersfromafrica.blogspot.com

This book has caused me to look at my grandparenting style to a degree that I never have before. I am not an uninvolved grandparent. In fact I think of myself as a pretty good one. For years I've known that all our grandchildren are at risk of losing everything, even their very souls. But now our tumultuous culture is at the apex of its very tipping point. And I've taken a too-easy road in the past. That changes-right now! My grandchildren are one of God's most important gifts. Cavin aptly and passionately says, "There's a battle raging for the hearts and minds of our grandchildren. The enemy is intent on destroying their souls. God's grand call is for grandparents to engage that enemy and fight for their souls." I'm now absolutely convinced that's what courageous, radically loving grandparents must do. My full armor is now on. I will not give up one more inch or moment being passive about what is my most important role in my grandchildren's lives. I urge you to read this important book. Then act upon its critical and timely message. Your grandchildren's lives depend on it. And time is running out!"

—JANE TERRY, President TresMark Communications; Denver, CO

Cavin Harper has issued an urgent call for courageous grandparenting in the turbulent times we live in today. He compares this call to Nehemiah's call to rebuild the temple and fight for the faith for our families. Baby Boomer grandparents and beyond are urged to wake up, wise up, and rise up to their God given responsibility. Christian grandparents have a sacred trust to co-partner with God to pass His faithfulness on to their future generations. As a result of reading this book, you will gain a fresh view of what it means to be an intentional, radical Christian grandparent for our time."

—LILLIAN PENNER, National Prayer Coordinator for Christian Grandparenting Network; Author of *Grandparenting with a Purpose*

Courageous Grandparenting is a "must read" for every Christian grandparent who wants to make a difference in the lives of their grandchildren. Cavin's intentional, relevant, motivating approach with common sense suggestions will make you wonder why you haven't been doing those things from the day you first knew a "little one" was going to join your family. This book will forever change the way you view your responsibilities as a grandparent."

—LANA ROCKWELL, author of *Passing On A Written Legacy*; www. mymemoriesforyou.net

Table of Contents

Introduction

Life is not often what it seems. In the village of Fairwater life couldn't be better—so it seemed. Fairwater's story is our story. It's a story of ordinary people, like you and me, who may saunder through life with few expectations of it being anything but good.

Nestled at the northern edge of a lush mountain valley accented by dazzling colors of alpine flora, the village of Fairwater sits in all its glory. Towering snow-capped mountains rise like watchful guardians of a magical panorama of grassy meadows and jeweled flora.

High in these magnificent mountains lives a kind and hospitable hermit named Josef. Josef is the Keeper of the Spring for Fairwater. His job is to keep the wellspring that supplies the village's most precious commodity and source of its prosperity—its water. Josef faithfully performs his duties as he has done for longer than anyone can remember.

The spring Josef protects produces sweet, refreshing water unlike any other in the region. Vacationers, health seekers, fishermen and merchants alike come from throughout the kingdom to savor Fairwater's delicious water. Many believe the waters possess healing powers. Visitors arrive daily to fill bottles and jars with the invigorating liquid pouring from the enormous public fountain in the center of town.

Village children rollick in pristine pools. In nearby Crystal Lake, fishermen enjoy the best fishing imaginable. It is not unreasonable to describe Fairwater as a place where life is perceived as *good*.

Josef did not often wander far from the cottage next to the spring where he lived. In fact, he had not ventured into the village for years, which explains why most people in Fairwater forgot he even existed. The few who remembered him never really gave him much thought. He was simply an old hermit living by himself in the hills. Few knew why he was there.

Which explains why the history of the wellspring once passed from generation to generation gradually was forgotten. It's possible a long life of ease and contentment in their peaceful valley accounts for the disappearance of that history. The good life of Fairwater was--how else shall we say it?--taken for granted.

It was inevitable, I suppose, that the need to keep a Keeper of the Spring so forgotten would be proposed. The Fairwater town council was no longer comprised of representatives with any knowledge of Josef and his duties. No doubt a responsible council would consider it their duty to remove unnecessary line items in its budget. Hence, the line item listed as "Keeper of the Spring" was deleted.

I suppose it was equally inevitable that Josef, after serving for so long, might yearn for something more. Hearing the stories of travelers ocassioning by his mountain cottage, he felt a longing to explore the world outside the valley—places he only imagined.

Thus, when the notice arrived declaring the Keeper of the Spring positioned ended, he wasn't greatly disappointed. Certainly, leaving the only thing he had known exposed a sadness he had not expected. Yet, a fresh excitement filled him at the prospect of a new adventure.

Still, he wondered who would take care of the Spring. *I suppose they must figure it out on their own.* With that thought, he packed his few belongings, locked up the cottage, and set out to experience life beyond the spring.

Things in Fairwater continued much as they always had… for a while. Then subtle changes occurred at the wellspring. At first, no one paid attention, even as piles of rotting pine needles and other decaying forest vegetation steadily built up around the spring. Trash left by the occasional travelers accumulated around the cottage and wellspring. For a time, the flow from the spring was strong enough to break through the accumulating debris and force its way into the stream channel.

However, the passing of time revealed gradual changes soon too obvious to overlook. The natural buildup owing to the cycles of nature caused the stream to finally yield to the build up around the well. As the stream channel slowed, the water from the spring gradually dispersed around the cottage creating a marshy bog.

Before long, people in the village people commented that water flow into the pools and town fountain appeared to diminish. As the water slowed, a peculiar greenish tint appeared. Many voiced their concern to the Village Council.

"We assure you it's nothing", the Council responded. "We still have the purest water in the region. There's nothing to worry about. We're sure this change is temporary. We have people looking into it. Everything will be fine."

Regardless of their assurances, it was not long before several children in the village complained of intense stomach pain. Many children became so ill they had to stay home from school. Doctors diagnosed it as a virus of some kind, perhaps brought in by outsiders. Confident it would run its course in a few weeks, they prescribed rest and yes… drink lots of water.

From there things only got worse. Not only were more children getting sick, a few died from their illness. Adults were not immune either, especially the elderly. Panic surged through the village. People demanded answers. The Council tried to assure them everything was under control, insisting it would soon run its course and everything would be back to normal.

Run its course, it did—but not as expected. By the end of the second year, the green hue and putrid odor permeated all the water in the village. Reports surfaced of dead fish along the shoreline of their once popular Crystal Lake. The water level in the lake dropped so much that the once pristine fishing destination turned into a swamp.

Fisherman no longer came to Fairwater. Tourists no longer arrived to swim in the pools or buy bottles of the famous water. Rumor spread that outsiders called Fairwater--*Foulwater*. The village was dying, and people wondered if it would ever return to what it once was. Despite all of this, the Council continued to assert that everything would be fine.

Their patience exhausted, villagers called for an emergency Council meeting. Tempers flared, as people demanded truthful answers. No one noticed the stranger quietly slip in and sit in the back. As tempers escalated, the stranger rose to his feet and asked to speak to the Council.

"I can explain the source of your problem and how to fix it."

"*You* know how to fix it?" scoffed one councilman. "Are you more knowledgeable than all the experts who have been working on this for almost two years?"

"Perhaps I am."

"Is that so? So, you are a hydrologist, then?"

"I don't think so. I'm not even sure what that is, but I do…"

"I see. Sir, I don't know who you are, but I thank you for your concern. This matter demands trained experts to resolve. I think we will manage just fine without your help."

"So it appears."

Villagers chuckled. Some voiced their agreement with the old man's perceptiveness.

"Sirs, I am not one of those fancy-titled experts you mentioned—hydro… whatever. But, I can explain the cause of the problem and how to fix it… if you're interested."

Before the Council could respond, one villager jumped to his feet.

"We want to hear what he has to say. You keep promising us solutions, but nothing improves. It only gets worse. What have we got to lose? Let him speak!"

The crowd shouted their support, forcing the Council to relent. They granted him five minutes to say what he had to say.

"The problem is not complicated and neither is the solution," he began. "Both relate to a decision this Council made two years ago to cut a vital position this village needs. You must restore the Keeper of the Spring."

"The what?" a councilman asked.

"Have you forgotten so soon? The Keeper of the Spring is essential for this village. It has been since it was founded. But the Council decided two years ago that it was an unnecessary cost. Had they done their research, they would have discovered that long ago the founders of this village considered it important enough to secure the King's royal decree. The Keeper's absence is why the water is bad and why the children and the village suffer. Reinstate the Keeper of the Spring and Fairwater will soon have its 'fair' water restored."

Murmurs reverberated through the room as people tried to make sense of the stranger's comments. One older woman mentioned distant memories of stories about a Keeper, but no one remembered for sure.

The Clerk of the Council promptly searched through the old records of Fairwater and discovered the royal decree. The room quieted as he read it aloud. When he finished, silence floated over the room like a mist for several moments.

The rap of the gavel startled the crowd as the Council President stood.

"I am embarrassed and beg your forgiveness for having neglected something of such importance. I think we should call for a vote to reinstate the honored position of Keeper of the Spring in Fairwater."

Loud cheers filled the room as the vote passed without a single dissent.

Then, the stranger stood and asked permission to speak.

"I must speak the truth. The Council is not solely to blame for this mess. I am ashamed to admit that I am also to blame."

A low rumble echoed in the chamber as the stranger continued.

"My name is Josef. Most of you don't know me, but I was Keeper of the Spring for a very long time. But this old fool did not speak up when the Council voted to drop the Keeper of the Spring position. I should have warned them of the consequences. But, I didn't. I convinced myself that I'd done my duty, that I was unappreciated, and that I deserved a chance to do what I always dreamed of doing—see the world.

"But the truth is I neglected my duty to this village. Over the years, I isolated myself from you. I failed to keep the stories and history of Fairwater alive. Why would the Council remember the value of the Keeper of the Spring to this village? My silent abdication of responsibility to you and your children allowed the story so vital to this village to fade from memory on my watch.

"I realize what a fool I have been. Please forgive me for my foolishness, for abandoning my responsibility to pursue a meaningless quest at your expense. Consumed with my dreams, I failed in my duty and purpose. I am so sorry. I wish there was a way to undo the damage done and your personal losses."

As Josef turned to leave, a villager stopped him.

"Sir, you do not bear all the responsibility for our condition. Everyone in this room shares some blame. We were not careful to guard the story of the Keeper. We are all to blame. But that does not change the fact that you are needed in this village. We need you to be our Keeper of the Spring once again, but with one condition. You must form an apprenticeship school to train future Keepers of the Spring to make sure that the King's service for this village will continue for generations to come. And… I propose that the history of Fairwater and the Keeper of the Spring become required instruction in our schools. I can't think of anyone more qualified to help us tell the story."

Within months after the Council's decision to reinstate Josef as Keeper of the Spring, life in Fairwater improved. The pools and fountains ran clean and pure once again. The health of Fairwater improved once the fresh water from the spring cleansed the pools and village fountain. Over time the lake recaptured its reputation as a fisherman's paradise—much to everyone's delight. Once again, life in Fairwater flourished because the Keeper of the Spring resumed his duty.

***

I wish our story ended here. While clean water once again graced Fairwater's pools and fountains, the damage from protracted neglect was obvious in the village for many years to come. The grief of personal losses already suffered remained. The long-term effects of drinking polluted water would serve as a constant reminder of the reality of neglect, complacency and ignorance.

For Josef, his brief 'retirement' became a painful reminder of the consequences of selfish decisions. Some good came from it. Josef learned how empty the allurements of the world are compared to living out one's calling. He discovered that working unnoticed did not diminish a person's value or responsibility. The good news is that Josef realized he had only one life to live, and it was of no use to anyone to waste it living only for himself.

Most importantly, Josef discovered a vital truth. When one forgets who he is and why he is here, it impacts many more lives than just his own. Neglecting responsibility allows the filth of the world to strangle the flow of blessing and hope for the next generations. Josef resolved to never let that happen on his watch again.

What about your story— your village? Who is tending the wellspring of your nation, of your communities, of your families? Does it smell to you like something's in the water? It's time to wake up and reclaim our roles as Keepers of the Spring.

Preface

There was a light tap, tap, tap on my study door. Whispering loud enough to be heard, "Now who could that be this early in the morning?", the door slowly creaked open. At the sight of my smile, a grinning ball of energy burst in my office, then leapt into my lap, wrapped his arms around my neck, and squeezed. I squeezed back. No words were required in those few moments of embraceable delight with my then ten-year-old grandson that had become a frequent morning ritual in our home. I hope he never tires of the ritual. I know I never will.

I love being a grandfather. I enjoy being called 'Papa' and doing crazy things with my grandkids. As much as I enjoy the perks that come with being a grandparent, I have no desire to sit around and simply be a *good* grandfather. I am not content to be merely a good time for my grandkids. I want to live as courageously and intentionally as I can so they will understand the Gospel and choose to walk in the truth.

I hope I will never be guilty of trivializing or neglecting my responsibility as a 'Keeper of the Spring' (see Introduction). I don't want to be a barn-builder; I want to be a legacy-builder—the kind of legacy my grandkids will want to embrace and will outlive me for generations. I want

GRANDPAUSE I have no greater joy than to hear that my children walk in truth. (3 John 1:4)

them to see the glory, the goodness, the grace, and the greatness of God in me, and I want them to want it for themselves.

Whenever I watch network news or listen to talk radio or read an online newsfeed, it seems obvious to me that the world we live in is not a brave new world, but a broken, aimless world. It's time to pause our self-absorbed lives long enough to consider the consequences of the mess we are leaving for the next generations.

Evil times are nothing new in human history. Yet, there is something alarming about much of today's research suggesting a missing-in-action *black hole* of young adults who want nothing to do with Christianity or the church.

David Kinnaman, president of the Barna Group and author of *You Lost Me,* writes about this 'black hole'. "If you're an older believer, a parent, or a Christian leader, I am not pointing the finger of blame at you. Instead, I want us to recognize together our collective calling to love, accept, and partner with this next generation. That's not easy…we have to admit that we have messed up too often, attempted the impossible by our own effort, and missed divine moments of opportunity. *But we don't have to miss the next ones (italics mine).*"[1]

Kinnaman is right…we don't have to miss the next ones, but we will if we are not courageous and intentional about our responsibility before God. When I originally wrote this book, (first entitled *Not On Our Watch: Courageous Grandparenting in a Turbulent World*), I hoped to provide a few practical ways grandparents could build the kind of legacy that ought to outlive them. My intent was to challenge grandparents to take seriously their responsibility to tell the next generations the truth about God and the Gospel of Jesus Christ. We are, as Dr. John Piper explains it, to live our lives "making much of Christ in our lives as our all-satisfying delight so that our children and grandchildren will know the truth and desire to walk in it as well."[2] I am sure you would agree there is no greater joy for a parent or grandparent than to see their children walking in the truth.

The fact is we have messed up on numerous fronts. So, the question is, are we willing to step back long enough to see the big picture and what it means for the next generations? Are we able to see the sin that has led to the condition of the world we helped create, and own it as our sin? Do we have the courageous to change our family paradigm and bring it back under the direction and authority of scripture rather than culture for the sake of the next generations?

Some will deny the problem is theirs. Some will seek to blame others. Neither approach offers the prospect of a solution. Those who own up to their sin, repent, and surrender to God's grace and power to fight for their families, will serve as conduits of hope for this generation. They will open the door for God to do more than we could ever imagine for His glory.

Something similar happened in Joshua's time as well. After he and all those brave leaders who led the conquest of the Promised Land died, the generations after them did not know or follow the Lord. How did that happen? When I look at my generation, I can't help but wonder if history may, in fact, be repeating itself.

I will confess that I'm not a perfect grandparent. I make some of the same mistakes as a grandparent that I made as a parent. I often question why God called me to write this book and start the Christian Grandparenting Network. I have more than my share of messed-up stuff in my life and family. I feel the angst Moses must have felt when God asked him to be His spokesman in Egypt. I understand Moses' hesitance. Why would anyone listen to me, Lord, since I, too, speak with faltering lips?

For purposes only God knows, He has not released me from the assignment He gave me. In fact, He has opened new avenues of ministry and service I never could have imagined. Despite my limitations, I am compelled to stay the course, determined to learn from my mistakes, and driven to call upon others to join the cause.

There is one thing I am resolved not to do. I will not let my grandchildren grow up not knowing the Gospel of Christ and the grace God lavishes on those who believe—not on my watch! I will not become a deadbeat grandfather who fails to speak the truth in love, or who loses the right to be heard because my walk does not match my talk.

If you are a grandparent, you know that few things in life compare to it. Still, as *grand* as grandparenting is, there are days when it doesn't feel so grand. I'm not so naïve to believe that grandparenting is always filled with moments like those when my grandson burst into my study. The dreams we hold for our families are not always fulfilled. For many of you, being a grandparent means living with mountains of heartache, discouragement, and disappointment. I pray that this book will give you hope and strengthen you so you do not lose heart.

I believe that most grandparents have a deep longing to play a meaningful role in their grandchildren's life story. I believe most parents want that as well. That's my motivation for writing this book. My hope is that when you have finished reading, you will know that you have a few appropriate tools to help you play out your role successfully—as Heaven measures success.

But make no mistake…the hearts and souls of our grandchildren are at stake. It is not enough to be convicted. There must be a sense of urgency to compel us to dare to die to self and our agendas. Only then will we dare to live the courageous life we were meant to live—life with a capital 'L'.

Courageous, godly parents and grandparents share a passionate commitment to do everything they can to help the next generations know Christ and wholeheartedly follow Him as Lord and Savior. They are not content to settle for the easy road. They want to make Christ look great in the eyes of the next generations. This book will unpack what that looks like in today's world.

At the time of this writing, it is estimated nearly ninety million grandparents live in North America. There are millions more around the world. Yet, what impact have we made on the younger generations. Have we stood by in silence and allowed the Father of Lies to inject his venom into our culture, hardening hearts to the truth? The world we have left for the next generations to inherit is filled with darkness, turbulence, and uncertainty. That's the bad news.

The good news is that these are also times of extraordinary opportunity. Courageous believers who display an unshakable belief in the Gospel of Christ and God's Word marked by compassion, authenticity, and humility, will become instruments of God for doing something radically redemptive in our world. Your grandchildren don't need *good* grandparents. They need and deserve *intentional, Gospel-shaped* grandparents (and parents)—those who dare to embrace the truth for their sake.

If you have picked up this book because you are looking for more fun tips for enjoying your grandkids, or how to be their BFF (texting lingo for *best friends forever*), you need read no further. I have written this book for those grandparents who have largely been overlooked in the church and society, yet are serious about leaving a mark—the mark of Christ and His Gospel upon their grandchildren.

Having determined to do all I can by God's power to keep my grandchildren from becoming casualties of the lies of this world on my watch, I have learned something important along the way. I have learned I cannot do it alone. This is a community affair; a generational responsibility. We need each other—parents, grandparents, and the Church.

I believe the Church is the hope of the world. It is God's tool through which all the generations experience and display the glory, the goodness, the grace and the greatness of God for the world to see. According to Scripture, such a display of God's glory happens when *"the whole body, joined and held together by every supporting ligament, grows and builds itself up in love, as each part does its work"* (Eph. 4:16). This is how the body of Christ—the family of God—was designed to function. It is our collective calling.

Courageous Grandparenting is an invitation for you to join me in a cause that is bigger than all of us. Together, through the power of the Holy Spirit, we can directly impact the eternal destiny of another generation. We cannot afford to waste our lives. It is time to seize the moment and live wisely while there is still time.

But let's be honest with one another. This will not be an easy journey.

The opposition is intense and relentless. The task can seem overwhelming and daunting. Nehemiah faced his share of opposition when he arrived in Jerusalem to rebuild the wall. So, we will draw from his courageous journey of faith to guide us in our mission to rebuild the walls of truth that lie in ruins today.

It will be a journey that is undeniably dangerous. There are no guarantees of the outcome. On the other hand, what could be more dangerous than sitting back, getting comfortable, and doing nothing to rescue those who are perishing on our watch?

~Cavin T. Harper
Founder/President
The Christian Grandparenting Network

PART ONE

WAKE UP!

The memoirs of Nehemiah, son of Hacaliah.

It was the month of Kislev in the twentieth year. At the time, I was in the palace complex at Susa. Hanani, one of my brothers, had just arrived from Judah with some fellow Jews. I asked them about the conditions among the Jews there who had survived the exile, and about Jerusalem.

They told me, "The exile survivors who are left there in the province are in bad shape. Conditions are appalling. The wall of Jerusalem is still rubble; the city gates are still cinders."

When I heard this, I sat down and wept. I mourned for days, fasting and praying before the God of Heaven.

I said, "God, God of Heaven, the great and awesome God, loyal to his covenant and faithful to those who love him and obey his commands: Look at me, listen to me. Pay attention to this prayer of your servant that I'm praying day and night in intercession for your servants, the people of Israel, confessing the sins of the People of Israel. And I'm including myself, I and my ancestors, among those who have sinned against you.

"We've treated you like dirt: We haven't done what you told us, haven't followed your commands, and haven't respected the decisions you gave to Moses your servant. All the same, remember the warning you posted to your servant Moses: 'If you betray me,

I'll scatter you to the four winds, but if you come back to me and do what I tell you, I'll gather up all these scattered peoples from wherever they ended up and put them back in the place I chose to mark with my Name.'"

-Excerpts from Nehemiah, chapters 1 & 2 (The Message)

—— 1 ——
A Legacy Worth Outliving You

My wife and I drove the two-and-a-half hours to the hospital after receiving the call from our son-in-law. We arrived and rushed to the room where our daughter, Alisa, was about to give birth to our first grandchild. Two weeks shy of my forty-ninth birthday my first grandchild, Thomas, would arrive. I was going to be there to experience it all—well… at least part of it.

As I sat with the paternal grandfather in the waiting room, my wife, Diane, walked in to deliver the news. Thomas had arrived. Despite some complications with his breathing, she informed us that our blue baby would be fine.

Gratefully, his Avatar-like blue tint quickly changed into a healthy pink complexion. Now that he is a young man, I sometimes tease him about his oxygen deficiency at birth. "It explains so much about you today," I tell him. He just grins and rolls his eyes.

I can't speak about your experience, but something happened to me that day Thomas entered our world. I experienced an indescribable wave of exhilaration. At the same time, I couldn't escape the reality that I was old enough to be a grandfather. How did that happen? I noticed no gray hair when I looked in the mirror that morning. Did I miss something along the way? (Now that he is a young man, I have nothing but gray hair when I look in the mirror. It's painfully obvious I am missing a great deal along the way— and have gained more in another way!) I was struck by the brutal reality I was now one of *those people*—a grandparent.

The remarkable number of candles on my birthday cake confirmed that reality. Fortunately, it was softened by the unexpressible delight of my induction into an elite club reserved for *people like me*. I carry my membership card with honor. I know some grandparents do not share my zeal, though I am perplexed by that.

I once encountered such a person at a senior adult expo event. He approached my booth when he noticed the sign about grandparenting. After a brief conversation, this grandfather said something for which I was unprepared. He said, "If I spend two hours with my grandchildren, it's more than I care to."

His comment stunned me. Did he really mean that he considered time with his grandchildren unwelcome interruptions? Could a grandfather truly be so self-absorbed to not want to be bothered by his grandchildren? It saddened me to imagine such a grandfather's legacy. Think of the consequences for his grandchildren, and the story that could have been written for their lives, but will not.

We are all part of a story involving our family and how we live our life. As a follower of Christ, you know the story God is writing through you for your grandchildren is irreplaceable. It's much bigger than you, or your family stories.

If we surrender to the Author's pen, imagine how that story might launch a legacy of faith and hope in your family – the Gospel passed from one generation to another. You have the power to never give your grandchildren a reason to think of themselves as unloved, unblessed, or under-valued. Give them a legacy worth outliving you.

That day I became a grandfather, I realized what a mess my generation was leaving to our grandchildren to navigate. I asked God to show me how to help my grandchildren know the truth and walk in it, even through my messes. I asked God to help me make sure my walk and talk facilitated rather than hindered their understanding of who He is, who they are and why they are here. I vowed to be more intentional about helping them know the Grand Story of the Gospel than I did with my own children.

There is no getting around it. They will have to choose between two kingdoms—the kingdom of God, or the kingdom of Satan. There is no alternative. I want the witness of my life to give them every reason to submit to God's rule over their lives, and not Satan's rule.

At the same time, I sensed God calling me to do something I had never considered. I had to make sure my generation of emerging grandparents understood what was at stake. If we did not wake up to the responsibility God gives us to tell the Story, authenticated by faithful lives lived as citizens of the heavenly kingdom, the consequences could be devastating.

We cannot afford to leave a legacy for the next generations not worth outliving us. What good is a legacy that fails to make much of the compelling truth of God's lavish grace, His unfathomable love and indescribable glory expressed in the Gospel of Christ? The only legacy truly worth passing on is one forever shaped by that Gospel.

Not in Kansas Anymore

The cultivation of a Gospel driven legacy could be hindered by ignorance of the world in which we now live.

Most of us remember the Hollywood film classic, *The Wizard of Oz*. An innovative film for its time, we found ourselves transported from ordinary black-and-white scenes to the dazzling technicolor landscapes of Oz. We were drawn into the intriguing and bizzare adventures of a young girl from Kansas named Dorothy. Swept up by a tornado, Dorothy and her little dog, Toto, are transported with their farmhouse to this magical world of Oz. Stepping out of the farmhouse into this strange land, Dorothy makes the rather obvious observation: "Toto, I've a feeling we're not in Kansas anymore."

For those of us born before the 1960s, the journey into the 21st century is not unlike Dorothy's tornadic jump from one realm into another. We know we're not in Kansas anymore, but not sure how we got here.

Much has changed in a short time and continues to do so at warp speed. Postmodernism, digital technology, global terrorism, and sexual identity are major issues dramatically reshaping our world and our culture. Like it or not, we live in a very different world from the one in which we grew up.

Some grandparents, and parents, have never stepped out of the past. They believe they can relate to their grandchildren's world with fifty or sixty-year-old ideas and ways of doing things. Others, trying to be culturally relevant, end up compromising truth to appear relevant.

Many grandparents prefer the role of BFF (Best Friends Forever) to being a grandparent (something equally true for many parents). Do we truly believe kids need, or even want adults as their BFF instead of someone who knows and truly wants what is best for them—according to God's definition of what is best? I don't believe they do.

Gospel grandparents, on the other hand, understand how to engage their grandchildren's world to point them to the truth. They *get* that the times have changed… dramatically. At the same time, Gospel grandparents are not shaped by culture. They live to shape culture. Scripture forms their worldview, not culture. They lean on truth and grace to guide how they engage culture with compassionate relevance and boldness.

Which grandparent are you? It takes courage to step out of the world of your childhood and youth and bravely take the plunge into the world your grandchildren must navigate. It's true, much has changed, but truth has not. There may not be a Wicked Witch of the East, but the Enemy is actively marshalling spiritual forces of evil committed to devouring and destroying our families. Grandparents, you are needed on the front lines.

As you boldly and audaciously step out into a strange, constantly changing world, you wll be confronted with brokeness. You'll see families whose children are without hope or purpose. You will no escape the frequent distortions conerning right and wrong. Confusion about personal identity, and a moral compass no longer aligned to true north will dominate the culture. The walls of righteousness have crumbled and the gates are burned. Hopelessness plagues this generation. It may look like the Enemy is winning, but he cannot. Remember this truth--"greater is He that is in you, than he that is in the world" (I John 4:4).

The Lord said to Jeremiah, *"Stand at the crossroads and look; ask for the ancient paths, ask where the good way is, and walk in it, and you will find rest for your souls"* (Jeremiah 6:16), We are standing at a crossroads in our day, and the Lord is asking us to choose the path we will take. We can take a trajectory that is filled with anger, complaining, and blaming others. We can choose to shrug our shoulders, and declare it's not our problem, or… we can take a different path—one that leads to rest for our souls, and the souls of our grandchildren.

I pray you choose the good way. Assuming you do so, I invite you to join me in choosing the good way through the example of a man who lived a long time ago. What was true in his day is still relevant to us today. His name is Nehemiah.

GRANDPAUSE Each chapter will conclude with a section I call GRANDPAUSE. This is a time for us as grandparents to pause for a bit to discuss the important points and truths raised in that chapter. Each GRANDPAUSE will include questions labeled Thinking It Through, and an Action Step suggestion.

GRANDPAUSE...

THINKING IT THROUGH:

1. What does a successful grandparent look like to you?

2. What you think it means to leave a legacy worth outliving you?

3. What are some of the lies we buy into that might derail us from building such a legacy?

4. Do you believe your grandkids prefer not having a grandparent who is their BFF? Why or why not?

ACTION STEP:

If you are in a small group, take a moment to pray for one another, asking God to make give His spirit of wisdom and understanding to each of you concerning what a legacy worth outliving us might look like.

2

First Things First

Nehemiah's story is a kind of scriptural sextant for navigating the turbulent seas of life as vessels of God's grace and truth. Nehemiah lived in exile in the powerful and pagan Persian Empire. The Empire did not care what he believed—only that he did his job.

He was cupbearer to King Artaxerxes, not the most sought-after job in the empire. The cupbearer was the poison-tester for the king. If he tasted the king's food and wine before the king ate it, and didn't die, it was a good day. That was his primary function for the king. Because he possessed such a trust relationship with the king, he became one of the king's most influential advisors.

His familiar routine was interrupted by his brother and others returning from a visit to Jerusalem. The Persian Empire allowed a few exiles at a time to return to Jerusalem. These men were among them. Returning to Persia, they brought a report about the news in Jerusalem. It was not good news.

When Nehemiah learned how his homeland lay in ruins, he had to act. He could not bear doing nothing when that which had been the symbol of God's glory and faithfulness sat as the object of disgrace and ridicule.

A Grown Man Weeping

Ponder his response: *"When I heard this, I sat down and wept. I mourned for days, fasting and praying before the God of Heaven"* (Nehemiah 1:4).

Did you catch that? Nehemiah wept. It broke his heart. Not the response we might expect from a 21st century man. I see much more complaining than weeping among 'Christians' over the condition of the homeland. When did you last weep over the ruins of the moral landscape around you?

Nehemiah's broken heart moved him to fast and pray. Pay attention to what he prayed: *"I confess the sins we Israelites, including myself and my father's house, have committed against you. We have acted very wickedly against you. We have not obeyed the command, decrees and law you gave your servant Moses"* (Nehemiah 1:6).

Hold on a moment! The situation in Jerusalem was not Nehemiah's fault. Why would he repent for something he didn't do? This was another generation's problem, right? Not Nehemiah's! Yet, his worldview led him to a different conclusion. He knew his people's sin was his sin too. All shared the guilt of sin against a holy God. He understood the curse of an unrepentant heart.

Repentance is not a much-talked about or practiced posture among Christians today. Have you ever wondered why? Perhaps, it is connected with how we view God.

Talk of God's love and grace abounds, but not much is said about fearing God. We respond to the language of forgiveness. We like hearing how God will love and forgive us regardless of our mistakes. But discussions about repentance are often missing. When it is brought up, it usually focuses on feeling sorry for doing something wrong. True repentance is much more than feeling sorry for something.

Repentance means to turn away from the horrible affront we are to the glory, goodness, greatness, and holiness of God. Repentance is the fruit of a weeping soul devastated by its egregious rebellion towards God. Nehemiah sat down and wept. So must we.

It is easy to hear the old stories and miss the relevance to our own lives. Nehemiah had an important position serving a powerful earthly king, but he was still a slave. He knew this king could end his life for any reason. Despite this, Nehemiah also understood something more important than all this. He knew this king's power was nothing compared to the power of the King of all Creation.

Knowing God meant knowing himself. How could he not repent for his sin and the sins of his people? This repentant heart freed him to be a vessel in God's hands and to witness the power of God unleashed to do things he could not imagine. He knew God was not only just, but merciful and that His promise to forgive and restore was not like the promises of fickle human kings or presidents.

Nehemiah did not pray for someone else to catch the vision to repair the city walls. He knew the responsibility was his, even while an exile in Babylon. Only God could complete what God laid on his heart to do.

The apostle Paul wrote to the church in Ephesus reminding them (and us) that *"we are God's workmanship created in Christ Jesus to do good works which God prepared in advance for us to do"* (Ephesians 2:10). Read it again. We are *God's* workmanship. We are not the master of our fate or the captain of our soul. We are mistaken to think otherwise. If we think that way, one day we shall in all probability find that we have steered our ship onto the rocks. Perhaps you already have.

Nehemiah understood the *workmanship principle* hundreds of years before Paul labeled it. He didn't worry about whether this assignment was part of his gift mix or not. He did not toss the matter aside as somebody else's problem. His comfortable role in the king's court did not keep him from taking on something outside his comfort zone.

Nehemiah's heart broke because of the news of his homeland. He never questioned whether he should do something. His understood the only obstacle to making a difference would be an unrepentant heart. He believed God's promise of restoration and healing to those who repent and turn their hearts to Him. So, he surrendered himself without hesitation, and prayed the same for his people. This was God's work. His work was to respond to the call to trust God above and beyond anything He could imagine or accomplish himself.

I Cannot Give What I Do Not Have!

The Gospel is Good News because of a single essential truth--we desperately need a Savior. Sin has destroyed our relationship with our Creator and condemned us as objects of His just wrath and judgment. We have no ability to pay the debt required for our sin.

The Good News is that Jesus, God in the flesh, paid the debt we could not pay for the salvation we do not deserve. That salvation is available to any who call on the name of Christ and receive His grace by faith [See Ephesians 2:8-9].

Why is this important? *Because I cannot give what I do not have.* Without this Gospel-life marker as evidence of my salvation and relationship with my Creator, how can I expect my grandchildren to know or desire the same for themselves?

Many people sit in church week after week believing themselves to be Christians. Yet, the "gospel" is little more than praying a prayer to receive a free ticket to heaven. Having gone through the motions, they believe all is well, but it's not. Nothing has truly changed.

For some, faith is little more than religious duty – I attend church, I pay my tithe, and I live a *good* life. Yet, neither view of the Gospel adequately reflects the reality of the Gospel.

Certainly, the good news of the Gospel is that we are 'saved', but salvation has two essential components. The Gospel demands both components. Hydrogen and oxygen atoms are both necessary to form water. The Gospel's 'atoms' are 'FROM' and 'FOR'. Without both the Gospel does not exist. Let me try to explain.

The Gospel is good news because Christ has indeed saved us FROM something. We are saved FROM God's just wrath and condemnation. For those who believe Jesus alone is the way, the truth and the life, the promise of eternal life guaranteed through the Holy Spirit. We eagerly look forward to our new home--a new heaven and a new earth restored to what God intended for us from the beginning. This is a critical component, but there is one more.

We are saved FOR something. Paul says it this way: *"You also were included in Christ when you heard the word of truth, the gospel of your salvation. Having believed, you were marked in him with a seal, the promised Holy Spirit, who is a deposit guaranteeing our inheritance until the redemption of those* *who are God's possession—<u>to the praise of His glory</u>"* (Ephesians 1:13-14). The second vital component is that we are saved FOR the praise of His glory.

The Gospel brings to life that which was spiritually dead. Having been made alive in Christ, we are freed to live in righteousness through Christ. We are new creatures whose hearts and minds are also made new. Our lives now offer a glimpse to the world of the glory and goodness of God. Our good works glorify God as the fragrance of Christ oozes from us to others. We naturally want to share the Good News of God's grace and mercy with others.

Followers of Christ live their lives so that Christ is exalted in all they do. Jesus calls it "bearing fruit". He says it this way, *"This is to my Father's glory, that you bear much fruit, showing yourselves to be my disciples"* (John 15:8 – emphasis mine). Bearing fruit is a product of intimacy with Christ (abiding), intimacy with God's people (loving one another), and an inner longing to tell others the good news (go and make disciples). It is the fragrant evidence of being alive in Christ, and obeying the one single command Christ gave us that is evidence of our salvation: loving others as Christ loves us (John 13:34).

So, here's my question, grandpa and grandma: What do your grandchildren see as evidence of this Gospel in your life? Do they see the majesty and goodness of God through you, or only lifeless religiosity offering little reason to care about the Gospel?

I assure you, your grandchildren will know whether you are a devoted follower of Christ, or merely a weekend 'fan'. It's hard to make much of Christ if the Gospel has no relevance in your life beyond Sundays. There won't be much of the fragrance of Christ if you love the world more than Jesus as your all-satisfying delight.

I often ask myself what I offer my grandchildren that would make them want to know, love and follow Christ with all their hearts. How does my relationship with Christ impact the worldview my grandchildren (and adult children) embrace? How is the Gospel shaping and driving the way I live? Does it give glory to God through gratitude to Him whose grace made me alive by faith in Christ for His purposes?

The Gospel shapes both my walk and my talk. It's true. Our talk talks and our walk talks, but our walk talks louder than our talk talks. How well does your walk match your talk? It's an important question.

The Gospel has everything to do with how we flesh out our roles as intentional, biblical grandparents. It's simply not enough to be good grandparents.

GRANDPAUSE...

THINKING IT THROUGH:

1. How did Nehemiah respond to the reports from Jerusalem? When was the last time you wept over the condition of your city? When was the last time you wept over your family or church?

2. Whose sins did Nehemiah confess? Why?

3. Does the explanation of the Gospel line up with your understanding of the Gospel? Why or why not? Consider these scriptures in your response: Ephesians 2:1-10; John 15:8)

ACTION STEP:

Ask God to give you a genuinely repentant heart for or any sin and misuse of the Gospel, and a receptive heart for what God wants to do through you. If you can, gather other grandparents together to pray for one another. Check out our resources at www.christiangrandparenting.net under PRAYER to help you in this process.

3

Lessons from the Theme Park

"He who disregards his calling will never keep the straight path in the duties of his work."
–John Calvin

It was the summer of 1975. Our daughter, Laura, turned five. We were on our first family vacation to California. It would be Laura's introduction to the ocean and the Disney Magic Kingdom.

Laura loved the ocean. She reveled in the feel of the sand between her toes and the gentle waves splashing her tiny legs. So many unfamiliar sights, smells and sounds for a five-year-old to process.

Disneyland is a sensory wonderland for a five-year-old. Stepping aboard the 'Atommobiles' at the *Adventure Through Inner Space*, Laura's eyes widened as we rode into a giant microscope creating the illusion of being reduced to microscopic size. She was enthralled by our journey through snowflakes, molecules and atoms.

After it was over, she wanted to do it again. But our time was limited, so with a reluctant child in tow, we headed across the walkway to another attraction. While standing in line, we were distracted long enough to lose track of our firstborn.

I don't know how long it was before we realized she was gone—probably less than 30 seconds, but it was all she needed. Discovering an empty stroller, we panicked. Frantically searching through the surrounding crowd, we saw no sign of her.

Knowing how enthralled she was with the *Adventures of Inner Space* ride, we went back just to be sure. The line was long, and she was so tiny, how would we ever spot her? My heart raced as my panic grew. "I see her," my wife shouted. I turned in the direction she was pointing to see our tiny five-year-old making her way to the top of the ramp where the crowd boarded the ride. Somehow, she had slipped through all those people without anyone noticing.

By the time I got to her, I was experiencing the mixed feelings of elation and the urge to wring her tiny little neck. But then, I remembered she was five-years old. I was responsible for her. I am the parent.

Fast forward thirty-three years. Diane and I are vacationing in Branson, MO with the family of our youngest daughter, Alisa, then a mother of three. We were all at Silver Dollar City. One of our first stops was a giant play center in the heart of the park. There were lots of fun things for the boys to climb on—balls to throw and roll in, and water cannons to shoot at one another. Everyone was having a grand time.

Soon it was time to move on. We all (so we thought) headed for another area of the park. Very quickly we realized that six-year-old Wesley was not with us.

Once again, the same panic Diane and I experienced at Disneyland three decades earlier gripped the four of us. We retraced our steps, checking the gift shop where the women had been, but no Wesley. My son-in-law and I ran back to the play area to see if he might be there. We looked everywhere. There were so many kids. Where could he be?

We prayed, "Lord, help us find Wesley, and keep him safe." A few minutes later, my son-in-law found him in the ball cage having a great time. He hadn't missed us at all. We were relieved that our lost grandson was found.

Losing Track

Even now, as I write about those two anxious events, my heart is racing. I had nightmares about those events for weeks afterward. Occasionally I still wake up sweating as those memories creep into my dreams. Today I look back with a thankful heart because I recognize the connection between those events and my roles as both a parent and a grandparent. We can easily be distracted and lose track of what is important.

What distractions cause you to lose track of your children and grandchildren in life? The consequences are much more scary and dangerous than losing track of them in a theme park. If you've ever found yourself caught up in the concerns of your career or retirement plans only to realize you've lost sight of more important matters, you know what I mean.

Sports, amusements, and even church 'ministry'—none of these bad in themselves—can distract us from greater priorities. How easy to lose track of our kids and grandkids because life happens… and we are distracted. We must not assume that youth leaders and teachers are watching out for our kids. It's a dangerous assumption and unfair to them, because that is not their primary responsibility. It's dangerous because one day, we may discover that we have lost them to something or someone we least expected.

Here's the thing. God never assigned the primary responsibility for training up our kids to teachers, pastors or youth workers. That was never His plan. He assigned that responsibility to parents and grandparents. If you doubt this, let me share my journey leading me to that realization, which seems so obvious now.

Two Epiphanies

At the birth of my first grandchild, two things occurred that radically changed my perspective about generational responsibilities. These unexpected epiphanies changed how my view of grandparenting forever.

The first came as I gazed into my grandson's cherub-like face in the maternity ward. In that moment I was reminded of something I recently read in Judges 2:10. *"After that whole generation* [this is Joshua's generation] *had been gathered to their fathers,* **another generation** [this is their grandchildren] **grew up, who knew neither the Lord nor what He had done for Israel"** *(emphasis mine).* As I pondered those words, a disquieting sensation invaded my soul. Could this happen again on my watch? Would Thomas' generation not hear the Gospel because my generation failed to tell them?

Remember, the "another generation" in Judges 2 were the grandchildren of those who witnessed all the miracles of the Exodus and followed Joshua and Caleb into the Promised Land. How is it possible their grandchildren never heard the stories about the wonders God had performed over all those years? It's difficult for me to imagine how these amazing stories of God's deliverance could not be told and re-told every night around the tribal bonfires. Where did the ball get dropped? How is it possible someone so close to the action would not know the stories?

The Bible doesn't tell us. It only says they did not know. All we know for sure is that another generation grew up and rejected the faith of their fathers and grandfathers. They followed gods of the surrounding culture, and did what was right in their own eyes. It's a pattern that has been repeated among God's people throughout human history.

The second epiphany which profoundly shaped my life path occurred when I received a t-shirt. That's right… a t-shirt. This t-shirt was emblazoned with these words:

Grandpa's To-Do List
1. Spoil 'em
2. Fill 'em up with sugar
3. Send 'em home

I hear you snorting. I did too until something unsettling began to stir within me. I knew there had to be more to grandparenting than what this puerile axiom represented. Something must be done to challenge this cultural perception of grandparenting lest my grandson's generation and their children grow up not knowing the Lord or what He has done for them.

These two incidents roused something in me which rejected the culturally acceptable position described by my 'Grandpa's-To-Do-List" t-shirt. I wanted to enjoy my grandkids, to do fun things with them, and even spoil them occasionally. But if that was all there was, it would not be sufficient. I wanted to be a 'good' grandparent. Yet, I could not shake the question: "Is it enough?"

My Personal Journey

My personal journey as a grandparent began with a desire to answer that question. I found few Christian resources from which I might find some answers. The dominant cultural message was about grandparents enjoying their grandkids. I discovered that any biblical teaching about grandparents was largely missing in the Church. The subject was not on the radar screen of any Christian family ministry organization I contacted.

Ten years into this journey, I found an Arizona based family ministry with a new book by Tim and Darcy Kimmel called ***Extreme Grandparenting***. It provided a more biblical view of *grandparenting* than most. It was a good beginning for published works addressing the topic from a biblical perspective.

Knowing useful grandparenting resources were scarce, it was time to do something about it. I turned to the one resource where I could find the answers—God's Word. I discovered that, despite the lack of biblical teaching on the subject in churches, God has a lot to say about the subject. Here would be the one source that would help me provide resources to challenge grandparents toward biblical intentionality. That's what this book is about.

The Biblical Mandate

The Bible has much to say about grandparenting. The Scriptures plainly declare the importance of grandparents, as well parents, in the raising up of children to walk in the truth. It is very clear that both parents AND grandparents are responsibile to tell the next generations the truth about God's Grand Story--who He is and what He has done.

In case you're not familiar with these passages, here are a few references regarding God's instructions on the subject. I've underlined those statements either implied or directly given to grandparents.

- (Deut. 4:9) *"Only be careful, and watch yourselves closely so that you do not forget the things you have seen or let them slip from your heart as long as you live. <u>Teach them to your children and to their children after them.</u>"*

- (Deut. 6:1-2) *"These are the commands, decrees and laws the Lord your God directed me to teach you to observe in the land… <u>so that you, your children, and their children after them may fear the Lord your God as long as you live</u> by keeping all His decrees and commands that I give you, and so that you may enjoy long life."*

- (Psalm 22:30-31) *"Posterity will serve Him [God]; <u>future generations will be told about the Lord.</u> They will proclaim His righteousness to a people yet unborn—for He has done it."*

- (Psalm 71:17-18) *"Since my youth, O God, you have taught me, and to this day I declare your marvelous deeds. <u>Even when I am old and gray, do not forsake me, O God, till I declare your power to the next generation,</u> Your might to all who are to come."*

- (Psalm 79:13) *"We, your people… <u>will recount your praise generation to generation.</u>"*

- (Psalm 92:12-15) *"The righteous will flourish like a palm tree… planted in the house of the Lord; they will flourish in the courts of our God. <u>They will still bear fruit in old age, they will stay fresh and green proclaiming,</u> 'The Lord is upright; He is my Rock, and there is no wickedness in Him.'"*

- (Psalm 78:1-8) *"O my people, hear my teaching; listen to the words of my mouth. I will open my mouth in parables. I will utter hidden things, things from of old—what we have heard and known, <u>what our fathers have told us. We will not hide them from their children; we will tell the next generation the praiseworthy deeds of the Lord, His power, and the wonders He has done.</u> He decreed statutes for Jacobs and established the law in Israel, <u>which He commanded our forefathers to teach their children, so the</u>*

next generation would know them, even the children yet to be born, and
they in turn would tell their children. Then they would put their trust in
God and would not forget His deeds, but would keep His commands. They
would not be like their forefathers—a stubborn and rebellious generation,
whose hearts were not loyal to God, whose spirits were not faithful to Him."

Based upon these few references, I can reach no conclusion except grandparents have a critical role in God's plan for family discipleship. Yes, these are Old Testament passages written specifically to Israel, but I see no evidence these are not equally applicable to all of God's people under the New Covenant. Our responsibilities are clear and non-negotiable. The consequences of not taking these commands seriously are equally clear--a generation that does not know God or what He has done.

I don't know about you, but I don't want that to be my legacy or the legacy of my generation--not on my watch. I do not want to be listed among those the Psalmist calls a "stubborn and rebellious generation, whose hearts were not loyal to God, whose spirits were not faithful to Him" (Psalms 78:8).

George Barna notes that while most parents **claim** to focus on what they consider the most important matters in life, sadly, helping their children grow in faith and spiritual maturity is not one of them. *"The dominant spiritual change that we have seen—Americans becoming less engaged in matters of faith— helps to explain the surging secularization of our culture."*[1]

Parents and grandparents share responsibility for teaching and discipling our children to know the truth and walk in it. There are so many distractions that would divert us from this task, we would do well to remember the lessons of the theme park. Courageous grandparents do not hesitate to do what is necessary to minimize those distractions so we are ready to help our grandchildren grow in faith and maturity.

If we neglect this duty, we risk leaving our kids and grandkids starved spiritually, ignorant of the truth, and heirs of a legacy not worth outliving us. None of us want that.

[Grand Tip: I highly recommend obtaining a copy of Dr. Josh Mulvihill's *Biblical Grandparenting* if you want a thorough overview of the biblical texts related to grandparenting.]

GRANDPAUSE...

THINKING IT THROUGH:

1. If the Scriptures discussed in this chapter are to be taken seriously, what difference does it make in how you view your responsibility as a grandparent?

2. What are some of cultural messages that keep grandparents from fulfilling these responsibilities? How do you respond to George Barna's statement?

3. What keeps you from be more intentional about fulfilling the biblical mandate we are given as grandparents? How can we help each other overcome this obstacle?

ACTION STEP:

Select one of the passages listed in this chapter and make it a matter of daily prayer over the next week asking God to show you how to be more intentional in matters of faith and spiritual growth with your grandchildren.

4

Good is Not Good Enough

A certain man discovered a canvas bag full of hardened clay balls while exploring a cave along the seashore. About the size of his fist, they appeared to be of little worth to anyone. Thinking they must be the handiwork of children playing on the beach, he surmised they may have placed them in the canvas bag, carried them to the cave to play, and forgot about them.

He took the bag of clay balls and continued down the beach. Walking along the shore, he amused himself by tossing the clay balls, one at a time, as far out into the ocean as he could. After several tosses, one dropped from his hand as he pulled it from the bag. It fell against rocks on the shore and split open. As he stooped down to pick it up, he saw something shiny encased inside the clay ball.

Excitedly, he broke open the remaining balls and discovered that each one contained a rare gem. In his hands he held a fortune. Suddenly the color drained from his face as he remembered all the gem filled balls he had foolishly thrown into the ocean   lost forever.

I've always enjoyed rolling on the floor with my younger grandkids. Those are special moments of squealing and laughing as the tickle monster makes his appearance. However, if enjoying fun things with my grandkids is the only trophy I have on the mantle, then it's not a trophy that will mean much in eternity. We cannot afford to throw away precious opportunities to point our grandchildren toward the one thing in life that matters—the Good News of Jesus Christ. As good friend, Josh Mulvihill, says: "Our grandchildren need the Good News more than they need our good gifts", or I might add, our good times.

We cannot afford distractions from worldly enticements and miss
what is important for eternity. God's concern is not whether we are *good*
grandparents, but how intentional we are about teach them to know, love and
follow Christ.

I know good grandparents love their grandkids. They love having a good
time with them and giving them good gifts. I do not doubt you are a good
grandparent. You may pray with your grandchildren at meals or bedtime
and take them to church with you when you can. You try hard to be a good
grandparent. Let me ask you: Is that enough?

Not according to the Bible. Remember, we are called to tell as many as
four generations the truth. We are to tell them about the praiseworthy deeds
of God, His power, and the wonders He has done.

Under the new covenant, *those praiseworthy deeds of God, the
demonstration of His power and the wonders He has done* are fully realized in
the Gospel. The good news is that God has done an extraordinary thing to
provide for our salvation through the sacrifice of His Son on the Cross. But it
doesn't end with the Cross, for the power of the Gospel is the Resurrection—
sin and death conquered once and for all—without which, our faith would
be worthless.

Courageous grandparents are intentional grandparents. What we are
intentional about matters. We can be intentional in the way we provide good
times for our grandchildren. We may try to teach them proper manners,
respect and politeness. They may learn from us how to ride a bike, drive a
car, and practice the piano. These are good things about which we ought to
be intentional. Intentionality is not restricted to matters of faith, but it is
compelled by Gospel faith.

Gospel-shaped grandparents embody a conspicuous intentionality that
goes beyond being a 'good' grandparent. The aroma of Christ is strong in the
life of Gospel-shaped grandparents. Their grandchildren are more likely to
seek a Gospel-shaped relationship with Christ when their grandparents are
Gospel-shaped grandparents.

What does Gospel-shaped grandparenting look like? Here are three key marks I believe ought to characterize such grandparents.

Marks of Gospel-Shaped Grandparents

Gospel-shaped grandparents are abiders, which means they are fruit-bearers. Jesus told us that those who abide in Him will bear much fruit. In fact, apart from Christ we cannot bear fruit. Here are three key marks of fruit bearing (there are many more) as Gospel-shaped grandparents:

1. **Proclamation & Instruction**

   I will speak to the matter of proclamation more in the next section. For now, let me repeat a quote I used earlier in this chapter. "Our grandchildren (and our adult children) need to hear the GOOD NEWS more than they need GOOD THINGS from you!" Why would I be reluctant to share the most important thing I should share with my grandchildren, yet allow the godless lies and perversions of the world invade our home? I have no greater privilege than to share the Good News with my grandchildren. The Gospel is the foundation upon which the rest of the building rests.

   Instruction is that building. It is laying brick by brick core truths of Scripture and training them to walk in that truth. We call it discipleship. In this age of relativism and secular humanism, our grandchildren need to know these truths and embrace them. Ignorant of the truth, they will lack the ability to detect and deal with the counterfeits.

   Instruction also means we are prepared to help them learn to discern what is false from what is true when questions and doubts arise. In the Appendix you will find some helpful resources to help you do that with confidence and effectiveness.

   Good instruction requires knowledgeable instructors. We cannot give what we do not have, or teach what we do not know. Strive to be a student of the Word. You don't need a graduate degree to know and understand God's Word. After all, the Bible was given to those with little or no formal education. He sent the Spirit of truth to guide us in all truth. That's better than a PhD.

Our grandchildren will not remain faithful to a faith they do not understand and cannot defend. Neither will we. Thomas had doubts, but the evidence was too strong for him to remain a doubter. You have the necessary tools to guide your grandchildren to the evidence where they can know the truth and understand how to walk in it. It's what Gospel-shaped grandparents do naturally.

2. Supplication

Gospel-shaped grandparents are praying grandparent. Just as our salvation is not our own doing, we also know we cannot wrestle against the spiritual forces and powers of this dark world in our own power. Only God's spiritual weapons, through the power of the Holy Spirit, can win those battles. We also understand our powerlessness to change hearts. That is the work of God. Much prayer, much power. Little prayer, little power. Look in the Appendix for some prayer resources we have available to help you.

3. Imitation

Paul makes an audacious statement in his letter to the Philippians. He says, *"Whatever you have learned or received or heard from me, or seen in me—put into practice"* (Phil. 4:9). It almost sounds like a dare. How can he make such a statement when he had already admitted elsewhere that he was the "chief of sinners"? Either he is a fool, or demented. He is neither.

Paul declares that everyone transformed by the Gospel ought to say to those around them, "Imitate me". Not because you are perfect. Paul already admitted that. No, he's saying, "Imitate me even in the way I deal with my messes and imperfections. Imitate what you hear me teach you because it is true, and you see it in action in my life." In other words, let us make sure our walk and our talk say the same thing.

If I mess up, and I will, put into practice what I practice—confession: admitting I'm wrong, and repentance: choosing to turn away from that sin and do what is right. Isn't that the response you would delight to see practiced by your grandchildren?

Only One Life

Courageous grandparents make much of Christ because the Gospel drives who we are and what we do. We declare with Paul, *"I hope that I will in no way be ashamed, but will have sufficient courage so that now as always Christ will be exalted in my body, whether by life or death. For to live is Christ…"* (Philippians 1:20-21).

This is not religious lingo used to prescribe a life of boredom. Paul is describing life lived to the fullest because the Source of life is our delight. Life with Christ is not a monastic life. It is life engaged to the fullest. The strongest and riches relationships happen when lives are shaped by the Gospel. Gospel shaped saints know a peace that surpasses understanding because they have a hope found only in the Gospel.

Sure, Jesus said we would have our share of trouble, but we "take heart" because He has overcome the world, and He promised to give us His peace—not as the world gives.

When my grandparents were alive, I remember a plaque that hung in their living room. It contained a poem by C. T. Studd:

Only one life
'Twill soon be past;
Only what's done
For Christ will last.[1]

Have you ever wondered what your grandchildren might say are the things you treasure most in life? Might they identify obvious wasted opportunities in your life, like the clay balls tossed into the ocean forever lost?

Some might reasonably argue that contemplating such things is a fool's errand—the kind that led George Bailey to jump off a bridge in the American Christmas classic, *It's A Wonderful Life.* Some will say it is pointless to entertain thoughts about what might have been? It serves no useful purpose. I disagree.

An honest evaluation of how I have lived and am now living my life is a healthy process. Because I only have one life to live, I am often challenged to ask whether my life makes much of Christ or something else. Like treasures in clay, what I throw away may no longer be recovered. I can do nothing about those lost treasures, but what about the few clay balls remaining?

God has a very specific role for you to play in His Story. There are plenty of 'clay balls' left to put to good use. You are His conduit of blessing and truth for your grandchildren. What He calls you to do is a matter of greatest urgency.

Since you are important to God's plan for making next generation disciples, perhaps it would be beneficial to examine two pivotal roles God mandates for grandparents. In the next section we'll examine those and how they play out in today's world.

GRANDPAUSE...

THINKING IT THROUGH:

1. Do you think of yourself as a "good" grandparent? What does that look like for you?

2. What did you glean from this chapter that would motivate you to intentionally be more than a "good" grandparent?

3. Which of the three marks of a Gospel-shaped grandparent do you do best? Which one is most challenging to you? Why?

ACTION STEP:

Be courageous enough to ask your grandchildren and adult children to share what they think you treasure the most. Does anything they say surprise you? What changes will you make?

PART TWO

STAND UP!

...The king then said to me, "What is it you want?"

Praying under my breath to the God of Heaven, I said, "If it please the king, and if the king thinks well of me, send me to Judah, to the city where my family is buried, so that I can rebuild it..."

So, I arrived in Jerusalem...then I gave them my report: "Face it: we're in a bad way here. Jerusalem is a wreck; its gates are burned up. Come—let's build the wall of Jerusalem and not live with this disgrace any longer."

5

Two Pivotal Roles: #1–Gatekeeper

"Three quarters of Christian grandparents do not have a clear understanding of their role, and operate closer to cultural norms than biblical imperatives."
–Dr. Josh Mulvihill, author of
Biblical Grandparenting

My eldest grandson came with a boatload of questions he wanted to discuss with us. He was struggling with what he believed about Christianity. Suddenly, a budding relationship with a girlfriend with some very different theological perspectives made him wonder what was true. So, he came, not with one or two, but fifty questions.

He wanted help understanding how the Bible explained these questions compared to what he was hearing from his girlfriend's background. I can't tell you how thrilled we were that he sought us out to ask the questions. I realized as we were working through this process how pivotal was this role of Gatekeeper God had given us.

Sure, I know there are special purposes at different stages of our adult lives to which God calls us. Yet, at each of those stages God calls *all* of us to get up, and take up the battle for the hearts, minds and souls of those who come after us. Our families, our churches, and our nation are under fierce attack today. To stand against the Enemy, a few walls need rebuilding around our families.

We can pretend everything is fine or that it's not our problem, but ignorance is not bliss and neither is complacency. Failing to embrace God's purposes for our life for the sake of the next generations is akin to throwing priceless treasures into the sea.

God's people have always faced the brutal and unrelenting attacks of the spiritual forces of darkness. We know *"our struggle is not against flesh and blood, but against the rulers, against the authorities, against the power of this dark world and against the spiritual forces of evil in the heavenly realms"* (Ephesians 6:12). It has always been so since the Garden.

Parents and grandparents both share similar roles, but the contexts in which they are performed differ. Most grandparents may not be raising their grandchildren 24/7 (though, sadly, it is a rapidly growing reality). Yet they often have the listening ears of their grandchildren in ways parents sometimes do not have. The point is, we must embrace these roles in whatever context or teachable moment we are given.

The two roles we will be discussing, Gatekeeper and Storyteller, are based in Scripture, even though they may not be specifically named with the role titles I use. You can't miss them as recorded in Deuteronomy 4:9…

> *Only be careful, and watch yourselves closely* so that you do not forget the things you have seen or let them slip from your heart as long as you live. *Teach them to your children and to their children after them.*

This verse screams parents and grandparents. So, let's take a closer look at the first role – Gatekeeper.

Keeping the Unwanted Out

The concept of a gatekeeper may be foreign to some, unless you live in a gated community. Gatekeepers have one crucial role. They keep what is unwanted out so those under their protection may live in relative peace and security.

Effective gatekeepers need a clear understanding of what is unwanted or unwelcomed. They must know how to identify something or someone that is unwelcome. They know they must be on their toes, staying alert to what is going on around them. They dare not grow complacent or distracted like Josef in the Keeper of the Springs parable.

When it comes to our families, our churches and our schools, a threatening laxness has descended upon our society concerning the unwanted lies and entrapments of the Enemy. There is a growing stench in the water supply.

Many parents and grandparents have chosen a more 'hands off' approach when it comes to teaching their children matters of right and wrong. We allow messages to flow into our homes that promote bad ideas and behaviors rather than righteous living. It's rather ironic when you weigh such permissiveness against the fierce actions we often take to safeguard our children and grandchildren from predators, or to minimize risks with safety devices like car seats and bike helmets for our children's physical protection. Too often, greater value is assigned to body protection than soul protection.

True gatekeepers have a grander perspective. They know the Enemy is roaming about seeking to destroy and devour anyone he can, especially our families. He is aggressively seeking to take their minds and hearts captive. That's why Moses began with *"only be careful"*. We cannot afford to neglect watching ourselves closely, giving careful diligence to our own souls, or the Enemy will find a way in and we will have failed in our duty as Gatekeepers for another generation.

With that in mind, here are two critical facets of a gatekeeper's (or if you prefer, Keeper of the Spring's) personal responsibility to the family and community:

#1: GUARD YOURSELF

Some translations of Deuteronomy 4:9 translate it this way: "Only be careful and watch your soul diligently." This isn't only keeping out what is unwelcome. It is taking deliberate steps to ensure four indicators of our soul condition remain strong: heart, mind, mouth and character.

By the way, I cannot keep my soul well in isolation. When I allow myself to believe the lie that I can take care of myself by myself, I am left exposed and vulnerable. Remember, pride goes before a fall. I need the family of God, others in my own family, and trustworthy friends to see what I cannot see and keep me on course in these four areas.

1. HEART…

"Above all else," we are told, *"guard your heart for it is the wellspring of life"* (Proverbs 4:23). Little by little, the garbage and pain of a fallen world will harden our hearts if we have not set up appropriate proactive protections. Before we realize what is happening, the wellspring is stopped up with emotional and relational destruction, and our hearts drift far from God and His truth.

Jesus said it this way: *"Where your treasure is, there will your heart be also"* (Matthew 6:21). If I do not diligently guard my heart from the siren calls of worldly enticements, or from angry responses to people or things that irritate me, my heart will grow bitter and hard, losing sight of the all-satisfying delights of knowing my Savior's love and grace in this fallen world. I will forget the glorious hope that awaits and now sustains me. An unguarded heart is a vulnerable heart.

One of the real dangers of old age, is how easily our heart can become hard. I call this the condition of *elderitis*. Elderitis describes an elder state of disconnection with other generations resulting in a loss of influence and respect due to a desensitized spirit, a hardened heart, and an absence of purpose. It is a condition in which the inner man is no longer being renewed, where vision is replaced by reminiscence, and wisdom gives way to folly.

How do you avoid eldertis? Stay in the Word, proactively engage with other generations, and stay close to people who will be honest with you.

2. MIND…

Paul wisely instructs believers to "take every thought captive to make it obedient to Christ" (2 Cor. 10:5b). Do not be deceived. We must diligently guard our minds against the lies and deceptions of darkness. Our salvation through grace by faith does not take us out of the world. That's why Paul urges us to *"not conform any longer to the pattern of this world, but be transformed by the **renewing** of your mind"* (Romans 12:2). It's one thing to be informed. It's quite another thing what we let feed our minds.

A variation on an old Aesop's Fable describes a hiker preparing to climb a tall mountain when he encounters a scorpion. The scorpion pleads with the hiker to allow him to ride on his should because his small legs would not allow him to make the arduous journey. Doubtful about the wisdom of carrying a deadly scorpion up such a long journey, the scorpion assured him he would be good company and he could be trusted if the hiker would only oblige.

The hiker believed the scorpion. "After all," he thought, "he seems genuine… a really nice fellow. I think the risk would be minimal. After all, he's just a tiny scorpion." So, he agreed, and placed the scorpion on his shoulder.

On the way up the mountain, the hiker and the scorpion enjoyed a very pleasant conversation about so many things. The hiker was pleasantly surprised at how interesting the scorpion was and how many interests they shared.

The time passed quickly and the hiker with his companion arrived at the top of the mountain. "Well," said the hiker, "I am so delighted I could enjoy your gracious company on the way up. It made my climb so much more pleasant."

"And I agree," said the scorpion. "I, too, enjoyed your company." Then, without warning, the scorpion stung the hiker in the neck with his lethal poison. Shocked, the hiker asked, "Why… why would you sting me after all we enjoyed together?"

As the hiker took his last breath, the scorpion replied, "You knew what I was when you picked me up."

None of us are immune to the same kind of folly. It's not hard to imagine rationalizing as harmless something that can do us great harm. The more we entertain folly and let it dwell in our homes and minds, the more its poison works its way into our minds and hearts. Before we know it, we are trapped by things we know do not glorify our Father. Anger, slander, malice, jealously, pornography... it all has a way of gripping us little by little until we are in fully in its grasp.

Television and social media can be like a scorpion on our shoulder constantly whispering its lies and filth into our minds. We rationalize it has no control over us. We know when to turn it off, yet we don't. Paul exhorts us to think about things that are noble, true, right, pure, lovely, admirable, excellent or praiseworthy (Philippians 4:8). What I allow to fill my mind, fills my heart, and ultimately, spews from my mouth.

3. MOUTH...

I doubt any of us would disagree that the tongue is a fire—a tiny spark that sets a forest ablaze. Those who know about forest fires and wildfires know how destructive they can be and how quickly they can spread. Just ask the people of California during the 2018 wildfires. A small fire in each instance suddenly roared into a powerful, destructive force difficult to contain and destroying homes, lives and a whole town. The tongue is like that.

Carelessness about what fills our heart and mind can easily lead to a wildfire mouth—coarse joking, foolish or careless talk, obscenity and cursing. On the other hand, when we learn to speak what is beneficial for those who hear according to *their* needs (Ephesians 4:29), we create a safe place for our grandchildren to be honest with us and want to hear what we have to say. If our grandkids matter, we will care about what comes out of our mouths.

4. CHARACTER…

Character is a matter of integrity. A person of integrity is the same person in private that he or she is in public. Character stands out in those whose way of life matches what they say and teach. *"[Timothy] will remind you of my way of life in Christ Jesus, which agrees with what I teach everywhere in every church"* (I Cor. 4:17). People of character have no need to pretend. They are the real deal, and those around them know it. They are willing to put the interests of others ahead of their own, even when the risk is great. The fragrant aroma of Christ is evident to all (2 Cor. 2:14-15).

I sat in the memorial service of man who had served as my pastor and "boss" in my first full-time staff position. Bob Frederich had been like a father to me, and he was a man of indisputable character and faith. My eyes filled with tears as each of his children and many grandchildren stood to speak of their father and grandfather. The common message from each of them was his integrity—he was the real deal, and many of his grandchildren proclaimed that they were drawn to Christ because the fragrance of Christ was so powerful and real in his life. What will my grandchildren (and yours) say about our character at our funerals?

#2: GUARD THE TRUTH

Gatekeepers not only carefully guard themselves, but they vigorously guard the truth. As parents and grandparents, we have been entrusted with the good deposit to protect our family from the Enemy's lies (2 Timothy 1:14). We are told Satan is like a roaring lion looking for any way to devour and destroy our children.

The reason Satan continually attacks our children, and thus, the family, is that he knows the family is God's specific means through which His kingdom would be reproduced generation to generation. His goal is to capture the hearts and minds of our children (grandchildren), and he knows he will do that if he can convince Mom and Dad, Grandma and Grandpa, to neglect their responsibility to disciple the children.

The Gospel is more than an Easter story about the crucifixion and resurrection. It is essence of the good news we proclaim. It is the story of God's plan for an intimate relationship with Him at Creation, the tragedy of our separation from that relationship because of our sinful rebellion, the amazing love and grace extended to us through the sacrifice and resurrection of His own Son to pay a debt we could not pay, to the final happily-ever-after chapter when our Maker and Savior fulfills His promise of a new heaven and new earth forever. Therefore, we must teach and defend the core truths that tell that story accurately. We must be informed about how the Story answers the questions about why things are the way they are. No other story can satisfactorily answer those questions.

Do not be deceived, worldview matters for it reveals what we believe about how we live our lives and why. The dramatic cultural shifts we have witnessed in recent decades are the product of swirling undercurrents of changing worldviews we fail to recognize and expose because we let our guard down. These undercurrents build generation after generation until like gigantic waves breaking on the shore, they sweep us away in the riptide.

For example, the notion of God's existence or relevance is constantly under attack. In the United States, we have moved from *One Nation under God* to censoring God from the conversation altogether, and it happened in a very short time. It happened not because the truth about God has changed. It is that the gradual undercurrents of evolution and post-modernism have slowly eroded chunks of a Judeo-Christian worldview shoreline piece by piece. It's happened as a movement of cultural champions in education, politics and religion have methodically inserted themselves in places of leadership. Ignorant of the consequences of this change in worldview, most of us have followed, or at least not opposed, the subtle changes until all at once the waves crash over us and our families.

All is not lost, however. God's truth is and will always be true. Therefore, we must diligently teach these truths to our children, grandchildren and great grandchildren. What are those truths? Here are five non-negotiable truths that we must teach our grandchildren if they are to walk in it…

1. <u>The Truth About God</u>: He is Creator of everything that exists, Sovereign over all, all-knowing, all-powerful, all-present, compassionate, the source of all truth and everlasting love.

2. <u>The Truth About Ourselves and Our World</u>: We messed up; sin is in the world because we listened to a lie, thought we could be like God, and rebelled. We have lived under the consequences and curse of that choice ever since.

3. <u>The Truth About Man's Need for Salvation</u>: God's holiness cannot allow sinners to co-exist with Him in a personal relationship. His holiness demands justice for the guilty. Since we are by nature sinners and dead spiritually, it is impossible for us to save ourselves. We need a Savior who will intervene on our behalf.

4. <u>The Truth About Redemption (Gospel)</u>: God's holiness also desires mercy. Only Christ, the perfect Lamb, could satisfy the debt payment for our sin so that His mercy might be available. Jesus' perfect life, death, burial and resurrection demonstrate His worthiness and authority for providing redemption for us. All that is required on our part is faith – to believe in our hearts and confess with our mouths that He is Lord (Romans 10:9).

5. <u>The Truth About Eternity</u>: Christ is coming again. Every knee will bow and every tongue confess He is Lord (Philippians 2:11). Yet only those who have by faith received the gift of LIFE will dwell with Him for all eternity in a new heaven and new earth. Those who refused to believe will spend eternity in Hell. That's the truth whether we like it or not.

Start Your Engines

I'm not really a NASCAR fan, but I remember watching the final laps of the 2011 Daytona 500 NASCAR race. Trevor Bayne, at twenty years of age, became the youngest driver to ever win this prestigious race. It was quite a feat in a sport dominated by the *old boys* of racing.

Today's grandparents are among the youngest and most active grandparents in western history… perhaps ever. Like Trevor Bayne, we are making our mark in a 'race' that was previously an *old boys* club. We may look younger and be more active than our parents or grandparents, but how will we fare in this new role at this stage of lie?

We must be willing to set aside our own script and follow God's script for this new chapter of the story He is writing for us and for the next generations. It is a story filled with surprises and challenges, but also rewards. The enormous challenges will require steadfast courage and unyielding commitment. If we put our trust in God and persevere, there will be reward. Most importantly, our grandchildren will be blessed. They will know the truth, and the truth will set them free.

Will we come to the starting line ready to race, sold out and intentional about making history by finishing well? Or will we go down in history as a generation(s) more preoccupied with doing our own thing, protecting our own portfolios, and pursuing personal comfort than being a conduit of blessing and truth for the next generations?

We're about to find out. So, grandparents… start your engines. This race is on!

GRANDPAUSE...

THINKING IT THROUGH:

1. Where are the greatest challenges for you in this matter of guarding yourself? Heart, mind, mouth or character? Why?

2. Why is guarding the truth so important for us as grandparents to undertake?

3. Describe your understanding of "worldview" using these categories:
   a. What you believe about God
   b. What you believe about yourself
   c. What you believe about the world
   d. What you believe about our need for salvation
   e. What you believe about the Gospel
   f. What you believe about eternity

ACTION STEPS:

1. Choose one of the four areas related to guarding yourself that you most struggle with today. Ask God to help you identify the source of that struggle. Write down one thing you will do this week to address it. Now, share it with someone else you trust (a spouse, a close friend).

2. Is there an area in the worldview categories above that you just realize may be distorting your view of biblical truth? Ask God to forgive you for your wrong thinking and to show you what is true.

6

Two Pivotal Roles: #2–Storyteller

*God gave us the power of story to build the faith
of future generations in Jesus Christ.*
–Josh Mulvihill

No one was a more masterful storyteller than Jesus. He had a way of teaching truth and zeroing in on heart issues like no one else. His stories (we call them parables) related to everyday life. They were easy to remember, though the meaning might be obscure to some.

The Psalmist wrote in Psalms 78, *"O my people, hear my teaching; listen to the words of my mouth. I will open my mouth in parables. I will utter hidden things, things from of old—what we have heard and known, what our fathers have told us. We will not hide them from their children; we will tell the next generation the praiseworthy deeds of the Lord, His power, and the wonders He has done"*. The Psalmist believes that story is the preferred means to telling the next generations about who God is and what He has done. It's still the case today.

The role of Story Teller serves a function beyond that of family historian. Storytellers do preserve family history. It is, after all, important how our ancestry influences who we are and why we are the way we are. It is useful to know about our roots. But there is more to the role of Story Teller than our family tree. We are called first to tell His Story.

Tell His Story

I mentioned this briefly in the last chapter. Proclamation is God's mandate to parents and grandparents. We can provide our children with a roof over their heads, clothing, food, and education, but if fail to provide what matters for eternity—the Gospel story and how it shapes our worldview—have we given them what is most important?

Why are parents and grandparents reluctant to tell the Gospel Story? There could be many reasons. In my work with Josh Mulvihill, Josh often reminds grandparents of four common hindrance factors he believes explain why the Story most important for children and grandchildren to hear is not told: fear, discouragement, wrong priorities, abdication. Let's look at each of these hindrances.

1. **Fear:** It is not uncommon to hear grandparents express their fear of saying anything about the Gospel because they worry about the possibility of rejection. Either they fear their adult children will keep them from seeing their grandchildren or restrict the access to them, or they fear the grandchildren will reject them. It is a fear founded, not in fact, but in imagined reactions.

    Suppose my teenage granddaughter never told me she played volleyball, or that she was one of the top players on her team, and her team was the second ranked team in the league. How would I respond if one day I happened to see her picture in the news with her teammates after winning a regional volleyball tournament? My response would likely be, "Annie, why did you never tell me about this? I would have attended all your games I could, and I would have told everyone about how well you are playing."

    Imagine her replying, "I'm sorry, Papa. I was afraid you would not approve, and I didn't want to offend you."

    With no previous indications of my being offended by her playing volleyball, such a response would seem utterly absurd to me. Any reasonable person would agree. It is an unfounded fear.

Unless you have been told, in no uncertain terms, that any comment from your mouth about the Bible, Jesus or Christianity is off limits, why would you fear telling them something so important? And if they do react negatively, make sure it is not because you are pushy or insensitive.

2. **Discouragement:** Discouragement is normal when the response to the Gospel story is not immediately positive and receptive. Children may seem disinterested because they are easily distracted. Perhaps you did not choose the best moment for sharing the Gospel story. If they show little or no interest in what you are saying, don't give up. Wait for a more opportune moment.

   Not everyone responded to Jesus positively, and many did not respond to His message until much later. We are not responsible for how or when a person responds. We are responsible for the telling. The Father is the Lord of the harvest, not us.

   Who doesn't want their grandchildren to embrace the Gospel as soon as they hear it. Be patient. The Holy Spirit's role is to convict. Do your part and leave the rest to Him.

   One of my grandsons rejects the Gospel and the relevance of the Bible. He was raised in a Christian home and a strong evangelical church. He knows the Gospel. It is easy to get discouraged at his negativity and not bring up the subject. I can't do that. I will continue to look for opportunities to share the Gospel message with him. He matters too much to me. I use text messages, personal conversations or occasional notes to keep him mindful of what is true. It is the power of the Gospel that transforms hearts, not me. I cannot change him, but God can. I will not give up... there's too much at stake.

3. **Wrong Priorities:** It's interesting how easy it is to talk with our grandchildren about things that interest them and us. There is no end of talk about sports, music, fashion, celebrities, amusements, career interests, and even politics. But when it comes to the Gospel, not much is said. Why? Because it's not a priority. It's not our highest treasure.

If you do not grasp the urgency of the Gospel message for eternity, lesser things will have the higher priority. Is it more important that your grandchildren like you or love the Lord? Are you more interested in helping them make the team, or entering the Kingdom? If the Gospel is not a priority, guess what gets left out?

4. **Abdication:** One of the most common false assumptions by grandparents is that they are not responsible for telling their grandchildren about the Gospel. That's Mom and Dad's job, and certainly the responsibility of the church. After all, isn't that why we want to make sure they go to church. I have heard numerous grandmothers say, "If I can just get my grandson to church, everything will be okay."

   It's not okay. The church is not primarily responsible for evangelizing your grandchildren. You are. It is wonderful you want to bring them to church, but it cannot substitute for your influence as you proclaim the Gospel in word and deed.

   This may be the most egregious of all the factors we've examined. Fear and discouragement are understandable, though not excusable. Wrong priorities are not excusable but can be unintentional.

   Abdication, however, exposes faulty thinking in which we are ignorant of the resulting consequences. The Scriptures are clear—parents and grandparents are responsible for the evangelism and discipleship of the children in their family. Family discipleship is the biblical priority for effective discipleship.

These are serious hindrance factors the Enemy loves to dangle before us. The last thing he wants is for us to take the Gospel seriously. But we must! God does not make us responsible to 'save' our grandchildren. He asks us to tell and teach, then trust Him to reap the harvest from the seeds we plant. We sow, He reaps.

Practical Story Telling Ideas

The story teller role must be taken seriously. It's not complicated. You can do it. You might even be surprised how easy and non-threatening it can be.

Below are several practical ideas you can put into practice. These suggestions are intended to stimulate your creative juices. Don't force it. Take a deep breath, enjoy, and let it happen as naturally as doing life together. Resist the temptation to quit trying when something doesn't work. Regroup and try another tactic.

1. Family Time: Family time means a place for all ages to gather together at one time, engage with one another, and hear how our story emerges from God's story. (Check out Family Time[1] resources Kurt Weaver created for grandparents)

   There are a variety of contexts for family time. My favorite is the dinner table or other mealtimes where we sit down together. Another effective family time is bedtime. This can be a powerful way to connect in a non-threatening setting and recap the day's events.

   There may be other family time opportunities that work for creating a safe place to talk about hard questions and to explore God's truth together. Family time is where each person values the other. That happens as we listen and create an environment that encourages open and honest conversations.

   Family time is a place to unpack what the Bible says without a formal lesson. It can be a time for a more structured Bible study, but it is mostly about learning and growing through participation, not lecture. There are few things more productive than reading the Bible together and talking about its relevance life in any setting.

2. Christian Holidays: Advent-Christmas and Good Friday-Easter are prime opportunities to tell the story of God's salvation by grace. Open the Bible and read the stories of the Incarnation, the

Crucifixion and the Resurrection. Talk about why this is so important to the Gospel story. If you have younger children, invite them to help you act out these major stories of the Gospel.

We are so bombarded with the world's messages about these uniquely Christian holidays, that we can easily miss the real messages of hope and grace. Ask God to give you His spirit of wisdom and understanding so you may guide your families toward knowing Him better and telling His story well.

3. Prayer: I applaud those of you who regularly pray for your grandchildren. While it is important to pray FOR them, it is also important to pray WITH them.

    Learn to sense those opportune moments to pray with them. Let prayer flow from those natural moments when you speak of God's faithfulness and goodness. They are ways to teach them to be thankful for His presence and grace to us in Christ. Praying is a powerful way to teach and tell.

4. Read together: There is an abundance of good reading available at the library, bookstores or online. Find those books you can read with your grandchildren beginning at a very early age that tell God's story and stir the mind to imagine with wonder and awe.

    I began reading the Narnia books with my grandchildren at a very early age. I then recorded a couple of the books so they could listen to my voice telling the story when I wasn't with them. They love listening to *The Lion, Witch and Wardrobe*, and talking about how Aslan is like Jesus.

    Lamplighter Publishing finds and reprints dozens of wonderful stories from earlier centuries that tell the Gospel story through the lives of children and other adults. Because the stories are written in and about a time in history that is so different from our own, they serve as great conversation-starters with children.

[Check the Appendix for additional resources for children's books you can read with them. These are stories that help you be a storyteller of the greatest story ever told.]

5. Audio recordings: Both Focus on the Family and Lamplighter offer an amazing selection of professional audio recordings presented in a radio theater format. You'll find information about these audio resources in the Appendix.

Everything in this list of suggestions is about taking advantage of teachable moments. Deuteronomy 6:4-7 reminds parents and grandparents to impress upon another generation what is most important "when you sit at home and when you walk along the road, when you lie down and when you get up." It's up to you to make these moments count. That's what intentional grandparents do.

Tell Your Story

As a Storyteller, not only do we tell His Story, we tell OUR stories. This is not as hard as it sounds. Children love to hear your stories. Your growing up years were much different than theirs. They often listen with wide eyes trying to imagine what it could have been like to live without smartphones and virtual reality.

The danger here is that we only tell the stories that focus on us. It is important to tell our stories in the context of God's Story so that the next generations not only know what you did and how you lived, but why you are who you are and how the Gospel impacted all of that. Here is what Your Story ought to include:

1. Family history: Ask your grandchildren to help you draw your family tree. Who are your ancestors? What were they like? What positive and negative traits have been passed on from generation. Use this activity to talk about the stories you know about Great Grandpa William

or Aunt Thelma. What have you learned from them? How have the people on this tree shaped who we are as a family?

2. Personal life and faith journey. How did the Gospel of Christ change who you are? What things are hard for you because of your family history? How did Christ and the Gospel help you to break free of some of those family obstacles?

Here are two additional suggestions for preserving your story:

- **Write it down:** Create your own family Legacy Journal or an Ancestry Album. The ancestry album records your family history and lineage of your family tree. You can include newspaper clips or old courthouse records that help tell the family history.

  A Legacy Journal features more personal stories. Part of the journal records personal family history (vita facts). The rest describes personal facets of your life (favorite vacations, pets, friends, embarrassing moments, engagements, school, etc.) and personal perspectives of life issues. *(See Appendix for resources to help you in this area)*
- **Record it:** With all the technology available to us today, it is not difficult to leave a permanent video or audio recording of your story and the legacy you want to leave future generations.

Story is so important to future generations. Some may say they have nothing to learn from the past, but without an understanding of the past, we cannot not know our own story and why it is important for today. God knew the importance of story. That's why He makes such a fuss about it. He knows the consequences of losing both His Story and our story.

GRANDPAUSE...

THINKING IT THROUGH:

1. What is most likely to hinder you from sharing the Gospel with your grandchildren?

2. Which practical story telling idea might work best for you? Which might be the hardest for you to use? Why?

3. What other ideas for telling your story or God's story might you have you could share with the group to encourage them?

ACTION STEPS:

1. Why is the factor in #1 above you identified causing such a problem for you? Ask God to show you the source of your obstacle to telling your grandchildren the Gospel, and to give you the courage to overcome that obstacle? Who could you share this with and ask to pray with you?

2. Decide right now how you will begin to tell your story of faith and important parts of your life story your grandchildren need to know. Don't put it off!

Allies or Adversaries?

Children's children are a crown to the aged,
and parents are the pride of their children.
(Proverbs 17:6)

Chelsea dreaded going to her mother-in-law's home for the holidays. Despite an otherwise good relationship, she knew visits with 'mom' could be tense. Most of the tension revolved around her mother-in-law's persistent violation of rules Chelsea and Dan expected to be followed with the kids. Mostly it was about what they could eat and their allowable bed time. Then there was the occasional unsolicited advice concerning childrearing.

If Chelsea said something about the rule violations, her mother-in-law reprimanded her for depriving the children of the fun things grandkids should enjoy with their grandparents. Chelsea knew the kids would eat any junk food Grandma put out. They would also be allowed to stay up late to watch TV or a movie if she or Dan did not put a stop to it. Chelsea resented the collateral damage they were left to clean up when they returned home. Why couldn't Dan's mother simply respect their rules and boundaries for the kids? Why was it so hard to work together on this?

Sound familiar? Okay, I know you don't see the grandkids that often so the rules should flex a little when they are at your house, right? After all, that's why the grandkids love coming to your house. They look forward to doing things at Grandma and Grandpa's they can't do at home. Do I sense some devilish delight in the old saw that says grandparents and grandkids get along so well because they have a common enemy? Payback time!

If you buy into that way of thinking you probably also buy into the notion that grandparenting is primarily about the grandparents and the grandkids doing *their* thing together. As tempting as it may be to take that approach to grandparenting, I hope to convince you otherwise.

Gospel-shaped grandparents know it is not just about the grandkids and them. Their top priority is to figure out how parents and grandparents ought to work together as allies, not adversaries towards the same objective— mentoring the grandchildren to become all God wants them to be.

A grandparent's job is to find ways to foster an environment in which our adult children can be the greatest parents possible. It's what courageous grandparents do. The moment we start to think and act independently or judgmentally, there will be trouble right here in River City.

There was a time when this God-designed alliance between parent and grandparent was a more typical family dynamic, though not without its share of ups and downs. Still, family life did have a kind of simplicity that is missing in most families today. Children commonly lived with one set of parents and two sets of grandparents. If the grandparents were still living, they often lived in the same community—maybe even next door. My wife and I both grew up in that kind of community environment. That is not the typical scenario today.

Getting It Together

A growing percentage of today's children have multiple sets of parents and grandparents, often separated by great distances. Divorce has dramatically changed the landscape of family dynamics. Grandparents must now cope with a myriad of complicating factors resulting from divorce and remarriage—and now, same-sex marriages.

Now that the family tribe rarely lives together, families often exist independently in their own cultural groups with differing values and traditions. This has exponentially complicated the ability to navigate this cultural mix of blended families and maintain family cohesion.

Despite these obstacles, the importance of a mutually supportive partnership remains unchanged. It may be more complicated, but it is still important and achievable in most cases. In fact, the need for such a partnership is made even more necessary by these complications.

It will always be true that a mutually cooperative partnership between parent and grandparent is one of the most satisfying and productive relationships on the planet. On the other hand, an uncooperative relationship with adult children and their spouses will likely unleash a tsunami of debris and destruction among family members in which few winners emerge.

Everyone knows, including the children, that the kids pay the heaviest price in incompatible family relationships. Conflict between parents, not to mention parents and grandparents, leave the children caught in the middle as mediators. That is not where children belong.

In Dan and Chelsea's situation, they knew something had to be done or things would only get worse…for everyone. In the long run, they knew everyone would lose if something didn't change. So, they chose to sit down together with Dan's mom to talk about the situation.

They were surprised to learn that grandma truly believed it was *necessary* for her to give the grandkids junk food and to let them stay up late. Why? Because if she didn't, she was convinced they would not like her or want to visit.

"It's what grandparents do," she explained. "They know they can do things at Grandma's they can't do at home. That's why they like coming here. Why deprive them of that? Besides, it's only once a year."

That revelation opened an opportunity for Dan and Chelsea to share a different point of view.

"Mom, we appreciate your wanting to give the kids a good time," they explained. "We want them to like you, too, but you're wrong if you assume how much they like you and being with you is determined by the quantity of junk food you stuff in them, or how late they can stay up. If what they eat and what time they go to bed is all there is to measure the value they place upon you as their grandmother, then something is wrong.

"These things have no bearing on how good a grandparent you are. They have nothing to do with whether they like you or don't like you. When you ignore and violate our rules we have set up for their benefit, you make us out to be the 'bad guys'. We promise you they will still like you even if you follow our rules."

I'm convinced that if more parents possessed the same kind of courage and profound wisdom demonstrated by these young parents, a great deal of family heartache could be averted. Their willingness to openly talk about the problem cleared the air and made it possible to lay a foundation for a mutually satisfying partnership that was a win-win for everyone, especially the kids.

So many conflicts could be resolved if the effort was made to talk about them with humility and honesty. It took a lot of courage for Dan and Chelsea to initiate that conversation and get the real issue on the table. They did it because their relationship with Grandma, and her relationship with the grandkids, was too important to ignore. Dan understood how important a grandmother could be in a child's life because his grandmother had such a profound impact upon him.

I am convinced most parents want their kids to have a positive relationship with their grandparents just as much as the grandparents do. For that to happen, somebody needs to step to the plate and put the ball in play. The conversation this brave couple had with Grandma ought to give all of us something to think about.

Will it really make that much difference in the relationship with your grandkids if you enforce some of the boundaries their parents feel are important while at your house? Obviously, some are convinced it will make a difference. I hope Dan and Chelsea's story will change your thinking. If violating parental rules creates the only positive connections you have with your grandchildren, something is terribly wrong for sure. Either there is a faulty thinking about effective grandparenting, or you are pathological. It might be worth some soul-searching, and then consider a different viewpoint.

Bite Your Lip

By far the most comments and questions I receive from grandparents involve their relationships with their adult children. Their questions generally fall into two categories:

1. How do I deal with hostility by one or both parents towards any open discussion about my Christian faith?
2. How do I cope with the resentment I feel when I'm around the grandkids and their parents, particularly in areas of discipline, rules, and parental boundaries?

Should you be one of those grandparents blessed with a positive relationship with your adult children and their spouses, guard that relationship with all your might, and keep it strong. For the rest, do not give up hope.

Many of the tensions experienced in our relationships with our adult children arise from differing philosophies of childrearing. There are times when I look at the way my own adult children parent and often wonder where they learned those things. Sometimes my wife and I see very little resemblance to the way we parented. That may not be all bad, I suppose, but the temptation is to step in and 'offer a bit of sound advice.'

There may be times when giving advice or taking even more drastic measures is appropriate and necessary. This is especially true in a potentially harmful situation. I can think of at least three areas in which such intervention may be necessary: 1) unethical actions; 2) immoral behavior; or 3) unsafe situations that have the potential for serious physical harm.

For example, it's one thing to say something if a small child is left alone without supervision in the bathtub; the safety of the child is at issue. It's quite another matter when that same small child splashes around in the dog's water dish while Mom's at home. That is not a moral or safety issue; it's a matter parental choice.

However, when it comes to personal preferences about parenting, housekeeping, or other personal life choices, most likely our advice would better be kept to ourselves. We would do well to remember some wisdom from Proverbs 10:19 – *"When words are many, sin is not absent, but he who holds his tongue is wise."*

We must not lose sight of the fact that our grandchildren could be the ones most negatively affected by any interference or potential rift that might develop. Wisdom is needed. Wise grandparents seek the parents' success in raising their child. We need to know when it's appropriate to speak and when it's time to keep our opinions to ourselves. Here's some advice about giving advice: *Don't offer any unless asked.*

Don't Lose Heart

There is no shortage of heartbreaking circumstances leading to conflict in parent-child relationships. Most grandparents, however, know that few things are more devastating than being torn from a relationship with a grandchild or grandchildren because of conflict with one or more parent. It's impossible to describe the pain of being denied the opportunity to see or communicate with a grandchild.

How does one bear the gut-wrenching agony that rips at the heart of grandparents who are forbidden to speak of their faith in any form around their own grandchildren? How do we find solace in the midst of the mountains of guilt that surround us when we know we neglected our own responsibility as a parent? Now, the fruit of that neglect feels like any hope for a positive relationship with that adult child and our grandchildren is threatened. What do we do?

There is no quick fix for any of these painful scenarios, but there is hope. The journey will certainly be a difficult and sometimes painful one. While the outcome cannot be guaranteed, in most cases, something good and positive can and will rise from the ashes of these crumbled relationships if we are willing to do what God asks of us.

If you are a grandparent embroiled in difficult relationships with your adult children, I want you to know that you are not alone. Let me say it again—*you are not alone*. At times, all that is needed is for someone to help you step back from the forest so you can see the trees—get some perspective.

My prayer is that God will grant you that perspective, and that you will trust Him by clinging to the lifeline of hope and grabbing on to the handholds of grace He makes available. Only then can you begin the upward climb towards a positive and productive relationship with your adult children and their spouses.

Never lose sight of the fact that the circumstances of a difficult relationship may be beyond your control. In fact, sometimes it has *nothing* whatsoever to do with you or anything you have done. But it does not mean *nothing* can be done. I plead with you not to lose heart or give up seeking resolution and reconciliation.

Perception Matters

It's true that perception matters in life. Whether we are to blame for something gone awry in a relationship, or not, is not the issue, unless we are too proud to admit it. What does matter is how others perceive the issue. When I understand that, I am better able to receive God's wisdom and grace to alter a perception—either because it is not accurate, or because it is, and I need to do something about it.

Only when I learn to understand and acknowledge another's perceptions can trust be rebuilt. When I am willing to address those things that may justify a negative perception, hope for resolving the strain in a relationship does not seem so impossible.

When my daughter went through a second divorce, I was devastated and angry. From my point of view, my reaction towards her was reasonable. From her perspective, my attitude and responses were condemning, unreasonable and uncaring.

I stubbornly clung to my pride for a long time. I convinced myself that, even though I disapproved of her decision (and I must be right), she had to know I still loved her. The truth is she wasn't sure I loved her.

Thankfully, my wife stepped in and reminded me that *my* point of view was not the issue. The issue was my daughter's perception. She perceived that my love for her was conditioned upon her measuring up to my expectations. Diane also reminded me that if our daughter continued to pull away, it could mean our grandson might be pulled away as well. Is that what I wanted? As hard as it is to admit, she was right.

After allowing myself to wallow in self-pity, I finally swallowed my pride and spoke to my daughter. I confessed that I had not done a good job of showing her unconditional love through all she had been through. Whether there was justification for the divorce or not, I wanted her to know she is my daughter, and I take great delight in her. I could never stop loving her or wanting God's best for her. I asked her forgiveness.

That was a huge turning point for both of us. By the grace of God, a relationship I had almost given up on was restored. And the added benefit was the preservation of my cherished bond with my grandson, who remains one of the great delights of my life.

While every family situation is different, the point of this matter is fixed. You have an infinitely greater possibility to influence your grandchildren's lives if you can maintain, as much as is in your power to do so, a strong, healthy relationship with their parents. Take that to the bank!

This divine alliance is a key component for keeping the pipeline of God's blessing unclogged. There is always something *you* can do to positively impact your relationship with your adult children. The wall of personal conflict can sometimes seem insurmountable, but with God nothing is impossible. We're the ones who are impossible.

The good news is that in His all-sufficient grace, He has provided us with five essential *handholds* to help us climb over that seemingly impossible wall of conflict toward positive relationships with our adult children—or anyone for that matter. Each handhold focuses on a specific aspect of godly character that impacts our relationships. As we climb and grip the handholds provided, what seemed hopeless can turn to hopeful. So grab your climbing gear—let's do some climbing together!

GRANDPAUSE...

THINKING IT THROUGH:

1. How would you describe the relationship you have with your adult children and their spouses right now? Can you identify in any way with the challenges Dan and Chelsea faced with their children's grandmother? How?

2. Do you agree that perception matters? Why or why not? How important is perception in being able to remove obstacles in that relationship?

3. What is the difference between enjoying your grandchildren and spoiling them?

4. How important are the relationships we have with our adult children? What are you willing to do to preserve and protect those relationships?

ACTION STEPS:

Sit down with your adult children, tell them you want to do everything you can to help them succeed as the greatest parents possible for your grandchildren, and ask them to respond to these questions:

1. What things do we do that make it difficult for you to be the parents you want to be?

2. How can we better partner with you to help you be successful parents and raise children that will have the chance to be all they are capable of being?

8

Get a Grip!

"A person's character is accurately measured by
his reaction to life's inequities."
–Unknown

Any experienced rock climber knows the importance of a good handhold whether scaling the side of a vertical cliff or an indoor climbing wall. A good hold versus a poor hold is the difference between success and failure in a climb—which means something very different on an indoor climbing wall than it does on the side of a mountain cliff.

A good hold, however, is only as good as an individual's grip. There are at least four other key elements required for a safe, successful climb:

1) **Using your feet like your hands.** You can stand on your feet a lot longer than you can hang by your arms;

2) **Using the right equipment**—no short cuts here;

3) **Having a trustworthy belayer** (the person at the bottom who holds the rope and is your lifeline should you fall). If you worry about the belayer, you can't focus on the climb; and

4) **Conquering your fears**; focus on where you're going, and look down only as far as your feet.

Good climbers have learned to put their confidence in their training, their equipment, their belayer, and the various holds and anchors in the rock. While fear is normal, they understand that if a climber cannot overcome fear, either he will be unable to continue the climb, or he will lose his grip and fall.

Life is a lot like climbing. Sometimes family relationships feel like you're standing at the foot of a steep mountain cliff with no expectation of being able to climb it. Yet, if we know we have the right equipment and that God is our belayer, we are free to stay focused on the climb. It now comes down to trusting the various 'holds' God has put in place for scaling the steep walls of relationships. He already promised that, *"His divine power has given us everything we need for life and godliness through our knowledge of Him who called us by His own glory and goodness"* (2 Peter 1:3). Believe it with all your heart. This is the source of our confidence to reach up, grab hold…and climb.

The following five handholds offer hope for scaling that seemingly impossible wall of conflict, and maintaining a strong partnership with your adult children and their spouses. These handholds are based upon Paul's instructions to the church in Ephesians 4. Paul gives us these secure handholds (he doesn't call them that) for navigating every relationship of life. Let's examine them briefly together.

Handhold #1 – HUMILITY

"Be completely humble and gentle…" (4:2)

Rick and Judy both use the word sensitive to describe his mother's relationship with their children. It's a word that expresses not only the way she conveys her spiritual heritage, but the unconditional love she always demonstrates towards her grandkids. "Even when they don't make the decisions that she might think they should, she loves them unconditionally. Her greatest gift to her grandchildren is to cover them with prayer every day," Rick observed. "Because of her humble, sensitive spirit, her grandchildren and great-grandchildren know they are loved unconditionally. I don't think there's anything either of us would change about how my mother plays out her role as a grandmother."

Pride and humility cannot co-exist. One is nurtured by the grand illusion of self-sufficiency and self-importance—a crumbling handhold that will lead to a fall. The other is cultivated in the selfless notion of losing oneself—foolishness in the world's eyes, but the surest handhold for a successful climb.

Humility insists on the interests of others over our own, and eventually leads us to see them as better than ourselves (Philippians 2:3). Sounds rather radical, doesn't it? Does that mean we should consider our children's parenting skills, or our perceived lack of them, as better than all our years of experience as a parent? Maybe—maybe not. But is it so unimaginable to consider that God has just as adequately equipped them as He did us to be successful parents for our grandchildren? Even if they aren't doing a great job (something we ought to empathize with), can we look through the clutter and give them our support?

Humility acknowledges our humanness with all its limitations. It allows us to rise above our humanity and rest in Him who knows better than we ever will. Acknowledging our own limitations frees us to own up to our mistakes, including our own parenting. Humility sets us free to admit that we may not have all the answers, nor do we always see things as clearly as we might like to think.

Humility liberates us in the security of God's grace to lay down our mantel of authority long enough to empty ourselves and extend the hand of a servant. Humility is the virtue of a grand-parent. Courageous grandparents are humble grandparents who respect and honor the boundaries of their adult children even when it isn't comfortable (assuming no imminent danger or serious injury exists).

It is foolish to bypass the humility handhold by insisting on doing things our way and expect to reach the summit of possibilities God has in mind for our family relationships—to the praise of His glory and the blessing of all.

Here are two scriptures all of us would do well to remember:

"God opposes the proud, but gives grace to the humble." (1 Peter 5:5)

"He guides the humble in what is right and teaches them His way," (Psalm 25:9)

Handhold #2 – PATIENCE

"Be completely humble and gentle; be patient, bearing with one another…"
(Ephesians 4:2)

The farmer who grows and harvests the Chinese bamboo tree understands patience. He knows that his reward for watering and fertilizing efforts during the first year will yield nothing more than a tiny sprout barely an inch high. Throughout the second year there are no signs of growth. The seasons come and go for another three years, and still the farmer has nothing to show for all his hours of labor with this stubborn tree.

In the fifth year, however, the farmer's patience pays off. Just when he might be tempted to lay down the watering can and give up, that tiny sprout suddenly grows at an astonishing rate. Before the end of that year's growing season, the tree that showed no signs of life for five years will soar up to sixty feet—that's six stories in less than a year!

Now, I am not a particularly patient person. Just ask my family. I like to see results—right now! I need constant reminders that truly important things in life often require enormous amounts of patience. Unfortunately, you and I live in a quick-fix world and have been trained to expect what we want when we want it. Whether losing weight, recovering from an injury or illness, getting service at a restaurant, or getting through rush hour traffic, we want it fast. When it comes to dealing with fractured relationships, it is tempting to be equally impatient.

Proverbs 15:18 says, *"A hot-tempered man stirs up dissension, but a patient man calms a quarrel."* Ouch! If patience can be such a powerful healing agent, why do I so impatiently react when things don't progress the way I want?

Perhaps Paul provides a clue in Colossians 3 when he explains that patience is the offspring of holiness and forgiveness clothed in kindness, gentleness, compassion, and humility. It's a worldview issue—how I view myself and those around me. Patience exalts the worth of another rather than my need to have it my way. It rests confidently in the providential work of

God in others…and in me, in God's time.

Patience sprouts in the soil of faith where the roots of unshakable belief in God and His Word grow deep. It is confident in the knowledge that the work God is doing in me, and in my family, is good enough. I am an instrument of God's grace, but I don't make the seeds grow. Since I can't control the outcome, it would be foolish to attempt to fix things. When I do, it usually results in a royal mess, especially in my own family.

Even though we saw the Chinese bamboo to grow to sixty feet in less than a year, it really took *five years*! In that five-year period every drop of water, every ounce of fertilizer, and every hour of care the farmer provided made a difference. Deep in the soil, obscured from sight, a large network of roots had been growing so the tree would have a firm foundation. If the farmer had impatiently tried to make it grow faster, he would likely have undermined the root system necessary for it to grow tall and strong.

Flourishing growth is the fruit of patience and perseverance. It applies not only to growing a Chinese bamboo tree, but to people. As grandparents, it's easy for us to want to jump in there and fix things. Be patient… and watch God do an amazing thing when the time is right.

Handhold #3 – FORGIVENESS

"Be kind and compassionate to one another, **forgiving each other**, *just as in Christ God forgave you."* (Ephesians 4:32)

Forgiveness was the big issue that built a wall between my daughter and me after her divorce. It had become a personal issue for me. I harbored a great deal of anger towards her throughout the ordeal because of all the injury to our family, and the impact it would have on my grandson. If I were honest, I would have to acknowledge that I was more focused on my hurt and embarrassment than I was willing to admit. Even though I loved her, my unforgiving heart placed a barrier between us.

Deep hurt carried around in an unforgiving heart is like large stones constantly being stacked one on another until a massive rock wall is erected across the path of reconciliation. Soon a root of bitterness sprouts and begins to spread like a vine across the wall of the heart with an aggressive cancer. Allowed to grow it can be very difficult to cut out, destroying relationships and blocking the way to reconciliation. Forgiveness cuts out the roots of bitterness and slices through the web of malice entangling a wounded heart. It stirs a lifeless heart to life like tulips in spring. It tears down the wall of unforgiveness so that peace and unity can flourish.

It's easy to talk about forgiveness when we want to be forgiven. It's quite another matter when we are called upon to forgive another who has deeply injured us—the kind of injury that occurs when a son-in-law or daughter-in-law refuses to let us see our grandchildren. Paul makes no bones about it. We are to *"get rid of all bitterness, rage and anger, brawling and slander, along with every form of malice. Be kind and compassionate to one another, forgiving each other, just as in Christ God forgave you"* (Ephesians 4:31-32).

Forgiveness springs to life when two things happen:

1) I realize how much I have been forgiven; and

2) I acknowledge how much I need to be forgiven (the Bible calls that confession and repentance).

Understanding how much I have been forgiven frees me to forgive others with compassion and kindness. It also opens the door for those whom I have wronged to forgive me.

The best grip on this handhold happens when we identify the stuff in those relationships with our adult children and their spouses, kneel before the Father who has forgiven us in Christ, and ask God take away the bitterness and anger.

Say out loud, "I forgive __________ for the hurt I have received. I will believe the best, not the worst. Fill me with the same compassion you showed to me, Lord."

Can you humble yourself enough to ask God to show you where you have injured a son, daughter or in-law, and seek their forgiveness? Avoid making excuses or justifying yourself. Admit where you have injured another (even if it's only in their eyes), and ask them for forgiveness.

Forgiveness, like cholesterol-fighting medication for the heart, unclogs the arteries so that God's lavish and extravagant grace can freely flow through us and bring healing for everyone involved. Because we are forgiven, we are free to forgive, to love, and to bless. So, while an unforgiving heart will shut the door to healthy relationships, forgiveness opens it and keeps it open. I suspect you know what I'm talking about.

Handhold #4 – PEACEMAKING

"… Make every effort to keep the unity of the Spirit in the bond of peace."
Ephesians 4:3

My wife and I used to operate a Christian retreat center in Colorado on the west side of Pikes Peak. During the summer, we occasionally hosted family reunions. One large family came to the lodge because one person hoped it would be a way of making peace in the family. This family came with a lot of grudges and angry feelings towards one another. I wondered if we had stepped into the middle of another Hatfields and McCoys shootout. The 'reunion' was assembled by a young woman in the family who willingly paid the entire bill, so no one would have an excuse not to come.

I was impressed by this woman's desire to make peace in her family. She really did want to see the warring parties reconciled. She knew true reconciliation would require more than being somewhat civil to one another for three days. Real reconciliation is what she longed for, and I suspect she knew this would only be the first step in a long journey toward that end. It was worth it for her to get her family members together and start talking again. She put her money where her heart was to achieve that goal, even though she did not see immediate results.

When Paul wrote Ephesians 4:3, I suspect he had in mind the words of Jesus, "Blessed are the peacemakers, for they will be called sons [and daughters] of God" (Matthew 5:9).

I've discovered over the years there is a difference between peacemaking and peacekeeping. A peacemaker possesses an unwavering determination to find the path to reconciliation for the benefit of all. Peacekeepers are more likely to settle for the appearance of peace to achieve their own agenda than to pursue true reconciliation.

We live in a world where incivility and rudeness dominate the way we speak to one another, even in our families. Praise God for people, like the woman above, who modeled the language of peace. We need more unwavering peacemakers.

Peacemakers are not focused on themselves. Their priority is to honor everyone involved by recognizing the value of every person involved. They have an unwavering resolve to hold firmly to what is true, honorable and lasting. They do not care about 'winning', but reconciling. Peacemaking is built upon a foundation of trust through which God's grace transforms hearts and restores a family that flourishes to the glory of God.

What motivates peacemakers? It is compassion and the compelling of the Gospel of Christ. *"For the love of Christ compels us (controls us), because we are convinced that one died for all, and therefore all died… that those who died should no longer live for themselves, but for Him who died for them, and was raised again"* (2 Cor. 5:14-15).

What marks a peacemaker? Here are four marks of a peacemaker as they function in a conflict:

1. Peacemakers listen carefully and compassionately. They are not defensive or argumentative.
2. Peacemakers are not afraid to admit they may be part of the problem.
3. Peacemakers invite input from all parties about how to resolve the conflict and let them know their ideas are valuable.
4. Peacemakers don't dig up the past or focus on past hurts. They look for the things that will build up all parties in the conflict according to their needs.

Peacemaking is hard work. The most powerful tool you have in your peacemaker arsenal is prayer. Use it regularly to seek wisdom and the moving the Holy Spirit in you and your family. Remember… in Him alone is our hope for peace, not in our cleverness.

Handhold #5 – WORDS OF BLESSING

"Do not let any unwholesome talk come out of your mouths, but only what is helpful for building others up according to their needs, that it may benefit those who listen." Ephesians 4:29

Howie was born into a broken home. He was left with his paternal grandmother who raised him. In elementary school, Howie was quite adept at causing trouble. In fact, his teachers were eager to pass him to the next grade, even without passing grades, just to get him out of their class. His fifth-grade teacher, Miss Simon, predicted that five boys in her class would end up in prison. He was told he would be one of the five. The teacher was right about three of them. She even once tied him to his seat with a rope and taped his mouth shut.

Then he met his sixth-grade teacher, Miss Noe. She told him something that would change his life forever.

"I've heard a lot about you, Howie," she said, "but I don't believe a word of it." She began to speak words of hope and blessing into his life that had never been spoken to him before. She broke the curse of negativity and showed him that she cared enough to say, 'Howie, I believe in you!' From that life-changing moment, Howie discovered the truth about God's purpose for his life and the high value he possessed as a person created in the image of God.

As an adult Howie went on to become a well-known author, speaker, and professor of Christian education at Dallas Seminary until his death in February 2013. The impact of his life on others would be impossible to measure. Dr. Howard G. Hendricks was one of the most respected evangelical speakers and authors in the twentieth century.[1] In the words of the late Paul

Harvey, "Now, you know the rest of the story"!

The blessing is the final handhold that grips a heart and promotes peace and unity in family relationships. We'll deal with the topic of spoken blessing more in next section. For now, I want you to grasp the fact that the peace Paul speaks of here is proactive.

Words are powerful weapons for peace and unity. Gossip, complaining, and cursing produce dissension. Words of blessing—intentionally speaking well of another—promote unity and peace. That is especially true in our families.

Speaking blessing into someone's life never goes out of style or loses its power. That's why Paul wanted his readers to understand the importance of speaking blessing in this passage – *that it may benefit those who listen*. I think Howie could vouch for that.

God isn't interested in excuses on this matter. His command is straight forward concerning the 'wholesome talk' issue. In another of Paul's letters, he makes it clear that building up others involves getting rid of *"all anger, rage, malice, slander and filthy language from your lips" and clothing ourselves with "compassion, kindness, humility, gentleness and patience"* (Colossians 3:8, 12).

The words we speak have the power to bless or curse. Instead of expressing our *learned* opinion, perhaps we could put an arm around our adult children, look them in the eye, and speak genuine words of blessing. Tell them how valued and loved they are. Remind them how cherished they are to God, how He desires to pour out His favor upon them, longs to prosper them as parents. We have the power to speak blessing or cursing. It is the handhold of blessing that will get us over the wall.

Clip In and Climb

Don't expect this climb to be easy or the outcome guaranteed. Doing what God asks us to do doesn't mean all the bad stuff will automatically turn into really good stuff. We cannot control how our adult children will respond. They must make their own choices. We can only pray they will choose to engage the climb on the other side of the wall, and meet us at the top.

There are things over which we do have control—things that may trigger withdrawal or hostility by an adult son, daughter or in-law. That's what this climb is all about. We decide whether the relationship will be molded by humility, forgiveness, patience, peacemaking and blessing, or whether it will be characterized by arrogance, condemnation, impatience, posturing, and cursing. It's our choice. One set of handholds will hold in even the most trying conditions. The other set will crumble in our grip. It is important to get a grip on the right holds.

The apostle Paul challenged the strong believer in Romans 14:13 with this instruction: *"Stop passing judgment on one another. Instead, make up your mind not to put any stumbling block or obstacle in your brother's way."* Could that also mean a son and daughter-in-law? Hold on, there's more: *"Let us therefore make every effort to do what leads to peace and to mutual edification"* (vs 19).

Sounds like some pretty wise counsel for those of us who care about the relationships we have with our families. Making every effort means not giving up. It means we keep on climbing even when our muscles are aching and it seems the progress is slow.

Take a cue from the Chinese bamboo tree. Trust that God is doing a good work through us and despite us. It's worth the wait to see the relationship with our adult children suddenly spring to life. It's worth the effort to hope for that joyous moment when we can hold our precious grandchildren close.

Whether the relationship we have with our adult children and/or spouses is horrible, wonderful, or somewhere in between, the rope has been tossed to us. It is up to us to clip in and scale the walls that hinder those relationships with the handholds God has provided. There is too much at stake if we don't try.

Remember, we have everything we need for a successful climb. The handholds are strong. Our belayer, the heavenly Father, will never let go. There is no need to fear. So…grab the rope, reach up, and climb!

GRANDPAUSE...

THINKING IT THROUGH:

1. Which of the handholds discussed in this chapter are most difficult for you to grip? Why?

2. Why is humility the key handhold to begin the climb towards reconciliation?

3. Are there handholds not mentioned in this chapter you think ought also be considered?

ACTION STEP:

If you are in a group, pray for each other in the area of your greatest struggle with these handholds. If you are not in a group, find another godly person who will help you and pray for you in these areas. Then set up a plan for implementing these four handholds intentionally in your relationship with your adult children.

PART THREE

BUILD UP!

By the seventh month the people of Israel were all settled in their towns. On the first day of that month they all assembled in Jerusalem, in the square just inside the Water Gate. They asked Ezra, the priest and scholar of the Law, which the Lord had given Israel through Moses, to get the book of the Law. So Ezra brought it to the place where the people had gathered—men, women, and the children who were old enough to understand. There in the square by the gate, Ezra read the Law to them from dawn until noon, and they all listened attentively.

As soon as he opened the book, they all stood up. Ezra said, "Praise the Lord, the great God!" All the people raised their arms in the air and answered, "Amen! Amen!" They knelt in worship, with their faces to the ground. Then they rose and stood in their places, and the... Levites explained the Law to them... They gave an oral translation of God's Law and explained it so that the people could understand it.

When the people heard what the Law required, they were so moved that they began to cry. Nehemiah, who was the governor; Ezra, the priest and scholar of the Law; and the Levites who were explaining the Law, told all the people, "This day is holy to the Lord your God, so you are not to mourn or cry. Now go home and have a feast. Share your food and wine with those who don't have enough. Today is holy to our Lord, so don't be sad. The joy that the Lord gives you will make you strong."

(Excerpts from Nehemiah, Chapter 8—Good News Translation)

******

The Lord spoke to Moses, "Tell Aaron and his sons, 'This is how you are to bless the Israelites. Say to them:

> *"The Lord bless you and keep you;*
> *The Lord make his face shine upon you,*
> *And be gracious to you;*
> *The Lord turn his face toward you,*
> *And give you peace*[Italics mine]

So they will put my name on the Israelites, and I will bless them."
(Numbers 6:22-27)

9

Unleash the Power of Blessing

"God does not do anything with us, only through us."
–Oswald Chambers

"We decided to jump in with both feet!", Steve remarked after he and his wife returned from a blessing workshop I taught. They decided to implement the principles they learned about the spoken blessing in their own family. Thanksgiving Day was just around the corner. The whole family would be gathered. It was the perfect time to put their plan to work.

"We prayed each day leading up to our Thanksgiving gathering and made a list of all the special attributes and characteristics we had observed in each of our children and grandchildren. We prayed that the Holy Spirit would provide the right timing and location for this special occasion. And He did!"

The big weekend arrived and the entire family was present. Once the traditional Thanksgiving feast was devoured, everyone spilled into the yard for another family tradition—a game of flag football. Participants and spectators alike enjoyed themselves despite the chilly Minnesota temperatures. When everyone had enough football, cold and tired bodies yielded to the glow of a beckoning campfire. Combined with a good cup of hot chocolate, the warmth of fire and family quickly settled over all.

"The setting was perfect!" Steve recalled. "We shared how proud and fortunate we were to have a family like ours. With football fresh in their minds, we asked for responses to the question, 'How is a family like a football team'?

To our amazement everyone jumped into the discussion, even the three-year-old. Others shared about the different roles we each play and the importance of encouraging each other and working as a team. We could not have scripted a better introduction for our time of family blessing.

"One by one, each child came and sat on our laps. We spoke to each of them about a special God-given talent or characteristic we saw in them. The children listened intently—more intently than at any other time we could remember with our grandchildren. Something transformational took place in that moment. God's presence was among us and was felt by all. Even our ten-year-old grandson asked if we could do this again."

For generations, much of the Hebrew community has practiced the spoken blessing as an integral part of family life. Many traditional Jewish families still speak blessings over their children during Sabbath observances, Bar Mitzvah and Bat Mitzvah.

A beautiful picture of this practice is played out in the movie, ***Fiddler on the Roof***. The scene shows the family gathered for the Sabbath meal as Tevye and Golde sing the "Sabbath Prayer" over their daughters. The words of the song beautifully express the rich substance of a traditional Jewish blessing.

May the Lord protect and defend you. May He always shield you from shame.
May you come to be in Israel a shining name...
Favor them, Oh Lord, with happiness and peace. Oh, hear our Sabbath prayer.
Amen.
(Lyrics written by Jerry Bock and Sheldon Harnick)

The practice of spoken blessing has been around since the very beginning of human history. It's not just an interesting storyline for a movie scene. God's first act after creating man and woman was to bless them.

Genesis 1:29 says, *"And God blessed them, and God said unto them, 'Be fruitful and multiply, and fill the earth, and subdue it; have dominion over the fish of the sea, and over the fowl of the air, and over every living creature that moves upon the earth.'"*

Since the creation of man, God set the example for earthly fathers and mothers to speak blessing over their children. I believe a restoration of this ancient practice could save an entire generation of young men and women from self-destruction.

More than Words

Somewhere along the way the practice of spoken blessing has been largely abandoned. Most Christian families have never given it any thought. In all of the years of my parenting, I don't recall hearing a pastor ever preach on the subject. This lack of teaching may explain why it is so infrequently practiced in the Christian community today. Grandparents are in a unique position to start such a tradition in their family. It is a role we should be modeling and teaching to the next generations for their sake.

The effectiveness of the spoken blessing rests on the assumption it involves more than a rote recitation of empty religious words. Traditions devoid of meaning, purpose, and compassion produce no more effect than a fine mist sprayed into a hot, dry wind. On the other hand, sincere words of blessing spoken over a child can refresh the soul like a cool drink of water refreshes a parched throat.

To bless literally means to "speak well of another." When the recipient of blessing knows how deeply we love and care about him or her, the impact can be transformational, even when the same words are used over and over.

When I asked my wife to marry me, I told her then that I loved her. Suppose I said to her, "Look, I told you when I asked you to marry me that I loved you. That should be enough. I don't need to keep saying it." Do you think she would be impressed? I'd probably be sleeping in the garage at night.

No one tires of hearing "I love you" from someone who means it. The frequent repetition of that simple phrase has an amazing power to keep a relationship fresh and strong. In the same way, no child ever tires of hearing words of blessing when spoken with love and sincerity.

In 1986 co-authors Gary Smalley and John Trent first wrote about the importance of speaking blessing in families. Their book, *The Blessing: Giving the Gift of Unconditional Love and Acceptance*, describes the biblical elements of an effective family blessing:

> *"A family blessing begins with <u>meaningful touching</u>. It continues with a <u>spoken message</u> of high value, a message that pictures a special future for the individual being blessed, and one that is based on an <u>active commitment</u> to see the blessing come to pass."[1]*

This book should have awakened parents to a desperately needed and missing component of communicating God's love to our children. Yet, the message seemed lost on most. I wonder how much different the family picture would be today had we paid attention and heeded the call to restore the biblical practice of blessing in our families back then. I pray we are not too late.

The authors outline five blessing elements in their book. I have condensed those into three elements, which I believe adequately encapsulate the essence of the spoken blessing. This is not a complicated process. Anyone can do it if they choose to be intentional.

My hope is that you will grasp the value and importance of the family blessing in your family. Imagine the impact if thousands of grandparents across this land set the example of practicing this good work in their own families.

I have been teaching the principle of spoken blessing in our various ministries at Christian Grandparenting Network since 1999. It is a powerful means of communicating God's purpose and high value to each person involved. However, the purpose of blessing is not to build your grandchildren's self-esteem as a way to feel good about themselves. The purpose of speaking blessing is to be a conduit of God's grace so they understand who they are and how precious they are. It affirms their identity as an image-bearer of God.

The blessing serves as a means for a regular, tangible encounter with the transformational power of God. We confirm His gift of grace and His favor through the laying on of hands and speaking truth into another's life. Our goal is that those receiving the blessing may know Jesus Christ as their Lord and Savior, and wholeheartedly follow Him always.

A biblical spoken blessing incorporates three critical elements that unleash the power of God's grace in child's life. They are:

1. A SPOKEN MESSAGE of *high value and a special future*;
2. MEANINGFUL TOUCH; and
3. AN ACTIVE COMMITMENT to support the one being blessed.

Element #1: Spoken Message

Most people are familiar with the children's verse, *"Sticks and stones my break my bones, but words can never hurt me."* This old saw is a lie. It sends the wrong message. The truth is that words are powerful weapons when used either to bless or curse. Even the most thick-skinned man or woman can be broken by another person's damaging words. Some handle it better than others, but most of us have a difficult time handling verbal abuse. The words of someone in authority can be unusually powerful for good or evil in a person's life, especially a child.

There is a desperate need today for older adults who will engage with younger generations to communicate blessing in their lives. They need to grasp how much God cherishes them and has already planned a meaningful future in Christ. We all want someone to believe in us and stand with us on the journey. Your grandchildren are no exception.

You are in a unique position to speak life-giving blessings into the lives of your grandchildren as no one else can. You have the means through the Spirit's power to overpower the flood of curses flowing into their lives as you fling open the floodgates of divine blessing upon them. The key is authenticity.

Children and youth sense when someone genuinely cares. Only when they feel you care will they be able to receive the words you speak. Therein lies the power of the spoken blessing. The words "I love you" stir the heart with a powerful reminder of what is true. The words "May the Lord bless you…" have the same power.

Spoken blessing is not reserved for the gifted or the well-behaved child any more than genuine love is limited for those who are compliant and easy to love. Every man, woman, and child needs to hear words of blessing by those with significant influence in their lives.

What We Say

The substance of the words we speak is critical. Specific words of blessing spoken from a loving heart speak life and hope into the life of a child or adult. The biblical examples for speaking blessing cntail two indispensable truth messages:

1. Affirmation of a person's high value.
2. Imagining God's special purpose for them.

These truth messages remind us that every person is made in the image of their Father who made them. Our worth and our purpose is rooted in the fact that we are God's image-bearers. This is the glory of man over every other living creature in God's creation. No other creature is made in God's image. Without an understanding of this foundational truth, life is devoid of hope and meaning. Let's examine the two messages of the spoken blessing flowing from this foundation.

1. High Value

High value is not the same as self-esteem. Self-esteem is exactly what is says—esteem determined by what we think of ourselves. The source of true esteem, or worth, is not found in self but in our Creator. It is the esteem of God that gives us our high value.

When we speak a blessing over our child or grandchild, we are affirming that which God has already declared to be true. They are valued because their Creator made them in His image, not because they perform in a certain way. His love is an everlasting love.

He proved it at Calvary where he willingly paid the ultimate price for our rebellion. The blessing is a way to proclaim the glorious truth of the Gospel. It is grace alone, not personal merit, which gives a person worth and makes him/her a child of God.

The blessing often softens a rebellious heart through the touch of the Father's heart. It awakens the soul to the truth that our deepest desires are satisfied in Him alone. God sent His one and only Son as proof of the high value He places on each person. Among all of God's creation, only man is privileged to receive the highest value stamp of the Creator.

Do not minimize the importance of the high value we convey to our children or grandchildren when we speak words of blessing over them. The affirmation of our words confirming our love for them because of who they are, not what they do, is huge.

We do not cherish them by making them the center of the universe so that they imagine that all other life revolves around them. That is narcissism and foolishness. Our goal is to communicate that God's love for them and our love for them is based upon the worth God has given them as His child.

2. Envisioning God's Special Purpose

Related to high value is the envisioning of a special future, or purpose, God has uniquely prepared for them. Again, this is God's work, not our work. It is an affirmation of the work God is doing and has been doing in them since birth.

Our ability to see and communicate this work of God is partly a function of how well we know them—the passions, gifts, and interests already at work in their lives. We learn to imagine this future as we become students of our grandchildren by paying attention to the unique ways God has wired them. More than paying attention, we also encourage them to pursue that purpose in Christ, who alone can channel those gifts into good works that matter for eternity.

The goal is to express an expectation of success and accomplishment as God works in them. He is preparing them. He is calling them. It has nothing to do with worldly gain or a career choice we may wish them to pursue. Career is what we are hired to do. Special purpose is what we are called to do. God has wired each of us for His purposes, whether in the context of career or some other part of our life.

Our role as conduits of blessing is to acknowledge this wiring that God is gradually revealing. In effect, we are saying to them, "I believe in you. I believe God will complete the work He has begun in you as His workmanship" (Philippians 1:6; Ephesians 2:10). The spoken blessing encourages the cultivation of those things God is already doing.

The second element is equally important for communicating to the recipient of the blessing the authenticity of the message spoken.

Element #2: Meaningful Touch Connection

The subject of touch can be 'touchy' these days, especially when children are involved. Men are particularly subject to suspicion. Growing public concerns about inappropriate touch only exacerbate a reluctance among men to express physical affection.

Contributing to the confusion is an unspoken code among males that it is not 'manly' to hug. For many men, a handshake is sufficient. Despite this hesitance among men, I think a growing number of men are throwing off the hugging phobia imposed by these cultural expectations. I love seeing a man embrace his sons and other men with genuine affection. Obviously, this remains an awkward act for many men. The risk of being misunderstood looms large. Yet, without touch, a powerful element for connecting the affections of our heart in the spoken message is diminished.

Psychological research recognizes the power of touch to express, and sometimes intensify personal emotions, feelings, and reactions. The long-term detrimental effects of touch deprivation on human beings are significant. Touch deprivation can hinder the emotional and relational development of a child. The absence of this basic human need can produce a lifetime of dysfunction.

A child deprived of meaningful touch will often spend most of their adult life reaching for someone else's touch. Evil predators prey on those robbed of affection in family relationships. Parents of children adopted from orphanages where personal touch was missing or negatively expressed understand the negative impact it can have on a child.

We were meant for touch. Notice that Jesus did not simply speak words of blessing when He called the children to Himself. In the gospel of Mark, we are told that Jesus *"took them [children] up in his arms, **put his hands upon them and blessed them**"* (Mark 10:16). Touch is an important means of reinforcing a sense that we are truly loved and valued for who we are, not what we do.

As an accompaniment to words of blessing, our touch infuses our words with a power that authenticates the message in the mind and the heart. Like a kiss that accompanies the words, "I love you," meaningful touch adds a 'wow-factor' to our words of blessing. Either words or touch may be meaningful by themselves at times, but when knit together in an act of genuine compassion they deeply affect a child's (and adult's) heart. Touch acts like a sprinkler system valve opening the way for the flow of life-giving words into the pipeline that connects to the heart. God wants us to be that pipeline—the delivery system for His water of life to a thirsty heart.

Our Creator meant for relationships to engage this way. That is why the curse of sin is so devastating in our relationship with God. We lost the touch and intimacy with the One who made us for Himself. The restoration of that intimacy is why the Gospel is good news.

Through Christ's love expressed on the cross, God reached down, touched our dead hearts, and made us alive in Him. The intimacy we were created to enjoy with our heavenly Father can now once again spring to life.

The goal is to speak blessing into a child's life (or an adult). Check your heart. Be wise, humble, and gracious in every act. Inappropriate touch will destroy the blessing you want them to receive.[2]

Element #3: Active Commitment

Our children and grandchildren need and want our blessing, but they also need to know that we stand behind what we say. When they know we will be walking alongside them in the journey ahead, they will put more stock in what we say. As important as our words are, if that is all we offer, it will mean very little in the long run. We must show our commitment to them. A failure in this life commitment could negate any positive message we may have communicated verbally.

Knowing you are there for them and actively engaged in their lives will validate and awaken the reality of the blessing. Your active commitment will serve as a barometer indicating the degree to which they are loved and valued. When a child senses you believe in her because your life validates your words, a heart is stirred to life. It is then that the possibility exists to see that child become all God intended her to be. What better gift can you give?

Let me insert a few words of caution here. Active commitment is not pestering or pandering, nor is it imposing your agenda on your grandchild. It is not about making your kids and grandkids the central preoccupation of your life. Nor does it require that we be physically present throughout their life to be effective.

Rather, it is about heart-to-heart connection, taking a keen interest in their world, listening well, and celebrating key milestones in their life. Show them the respect they are due. Honor them for who they are. Show them what it means to value, respect, and honor others as well.

To assume a keen interest in their world requires a measure of grace. Grace means you don't try to force them to live in your world. Guard against the temptation to be their buddy. They don't need a crony or BFF (Best Friend Forever). They need a wise, godly, and transparent adult who will listen well and help them navigate the world in which they live. They want to know you are committed to helping them succeed, and to let them fail. They want you to live up to what you say you believe about them and God's special purpose for them. If you do, you will establish a legacy of blessing for generations to come.

Armed with this foundational information about spoken blessing, we turn our attention to the how-to's. The next chapter will examine practical ways to establish a blessing tradition in your family.

GRANDPAUSE...

THINKING IT THROUGH:

Read Genesis 1:27-28; Numbers 6:22-27

1. What is the purpose of blessing? What did God mean when He said that the blessing puts "His name" on His people?

2. Review the three elements of the blessing discussed in the chapter. What is the significance and importance of each of these in a child's or adult's life?

3. Have you ever received a spoken blessing yourself? If not, how might that impact your ability to give your children and grandchildren what they most need?

ACTION STEPS:

1. If anyone in your group has never been the recipient of a spoken blessing, someone in your group should step up and bestow a blessing upon that person as the Father's cherished treasure.

2. Talk to your church leaders about the importance of the spoken blessing and ask them to explore with you ways that void could be filled in your congregation.

3. Stand together in a tight circle with hands touching the shoulders of the person next to you. Allow your group leader to speak a blessing over you.

10

Speak the Good Word

When Diane and I were first introduced to the concept of the family blessing, our children were grown and starting their own families. I remember picking up Rolf Garborg's book, *The Family Blessing*, and feeling a little angry that no one had told me about this amazing tool when my daughters were growing up. I wondered what special blessings they might have missed because I did not know about this tool God provided to parents to bless their children.

We decided it was not too late to pursue opportunities to speak blessing over our kids. We believed there were still amazing opportunities to develop a tradition of blessing for the next generations--our grandchildren and great grandchildren. We began with the birth of each of our grandchildren writing and speaking blessings over them. We then looked for other ways to use the spoken blessing. That's what this chapter is about.

If you are part of a church community, you most likely have a tradition in your church of closing a weekend worship service with a benediction or blessing from your pastor. We once had a pastor who always ended the service with, "Let me give you the good word." That's a great phrase. It is a "good word" because it expresses the Good News of God's grace, goodness, and continual presence in our lives. The tradition of speaking a "good word" as a benediction or blessing over a congregation has been around a long time. A great deal would be lost if the practice were stopped. Why not do the same in our families?

While the three elements of blessing outlined in the previous chapter ought to form the basic structure for any spoken blessing, how you present the blessing is up to you. There is no command or instruction in Scripture about how and when to do a spoken blessing, but there are plenty of examples. How you do it is limited only by your own creativity and effort.

If you've never incorporated the spoken blessing in your family traditions, you may be unsure how to begin. Let me suggest two possible plans for making the blessing a new feature that can transform your family.

The General Blessing

As we learned in the previous chapter, the Bible records God's instructions to Moses regarding the speaking of a common blessing over all the people of Israel in the sixth chapter of Numbers. It is the only place in scripture where God commands the blessing.

> *"Tell Aaron and his sons, 'This is how you are to bless the Israelites.*
> *Say to them:*
> *"The Lord bless you and keep you;*
> *The Lord make His face shine upon you, and be gracious to you;*
> *The Lord turn his face toward you, and give you peace."'"* (Number 6:24-26)

This corporate blessing became a pattern for speaking blessing over individuals and groups for many generations. For some unknown reason, the Christian community never included it in the teaching of the church for families. The failure to speak blessing over our children may have some bearing on why our prisons are overflowing and why we have so many epidemic addictions in our society. Deprived of blessing, many are looking in dangerous and destructive places to find something to take its place.

The general blessing is a simple, powerful tool for laying a solid foundation of blessing in your family. It utilizes two of the three key elements discussed previously—a message of high value and purpose, and meaningful touch. Meaningful touch was usually expressed by the laying on of hands.

In the case of a large group, the raising and extending of the arms and hands over the group depicted God's anointing touch upon them.

The only element not specifically addressed in the general blessing is the personal, active commitment, but there's no reason it cannot be easily added. When we examine the personal blessing, you will see that active commitment is an important element.

Before we dig deeper into this general blessing from Number 6, allow me to repeat something I stated earlier. The spoken blessing is a powerful way to regularly communicate important truths about God's personal care and favor on a child or adult. Some families speak it over their children every night. Many grandparents speak it over their grandchildren every time they come to visit or after a long-distance phone call.

How often you do it is not as important as doing it when the opportunity presents itself. Just make the commitment to do it.

There are three facets of the general blessing in Numbers 6 that I want you to know and teach to your grandchildren as you speak it. Imagine how this type of spoken blessing might be used with your grandchildren, your children, and other groups (a Sunday school class or a small group you lead, for example). Let's dig in.

Facet #1—God's Protection

The Lord bless you and keep you…

Singing in the Dark

In a world that often feels very unsafe and uncertain, God reminds us that He is Emmanuel, *God with us*. He will never leave us or forsake us. It is the Lord who blesses and keep, and God wants His people to remember that the hope and confidence we desire is found Him. He takes great delight in protecting us with His presence no matter how tumultuous, dangerous, or fearful our circumstances.

As a child growing up in Wyoming, my father occasionally took me and my brother camping at a place called Vedauwoo (pronounced 'vee-da-voo'). It was a fun place for young kids. There were large mountains of granite boulders surrounding several campsites and picnic areas. During the daytime, it was a blast to climb rocks and explore caves formed by the piles of massive boulders. For my brother and I it was paradise.

At night, however, things felt very different for two young boys. As the darkness enshrouded our campsite, the only light available was the fading campfire, and our camping lantern. On a cloudless night, the stars hung like suspended diamonds glistening in the sky, but they provided little comfort to dispel the fright of darkness. Even the soft, eerie light of a full moon brought little consolation as the shadows enveloped us.

The outhouse, an important resource for camping trips, was located no short distance from our campsite—at least it seemed that way to a small boy. The path to the outhouse passed through a grove of trees near a creek surrounded by two very large boulders. No matter how badly I needed to go, I could not be convinced to walk that path in the dark alone, even with a lantern. Who knew what lurked in those bushes along the path?

Fortunately, my father always came to the rescue. With the lantern in one hand, my hand in the other, we would walk down that path together. Sometimes he would whistle or sing a tune. It was usually a song from Johnny Appleseed, "Oh, the Lord is good to me…" Even in the face of terrifying darkness, I knew I was safe because my father was there with me, hand in hand, singing in the dark (which is even better than singing in the rain!).

The parent or grandparent who speaks this blessing over a child provides the equivalent of a song in the darkness. In those moments, if you teach the significance of this part of the blessing, a child will know he or she is in good hands. They will understand through your touch and words of blessing that the Father is with them—their hand in His—as He sings His song of love that drives out all fear, even in the dark.

Facet #2—God's Pleasure

The Lord make His face shine upon you, and be gracious to you …

Under God's Smile Umbrella

The grace of God is the ultimate expression of His pleasure in us who are His, not because of anything we have done, but because it is His nature to take pleasure in those He has bought with His lavish grace. The idea of His face "shining upon us" is another way of saying that God smiles—even laughs— because of us. To live under His pleasure is to enjoy His smile, knowing that He is pleased. It is to discover that in His pleasure we find our deepest pleasure. For the child (or adult) who lives under the umbrella of God's smile, there is no greater delight than to know that His smile reflects His grace in which He takes great pleasure in being gracious to us.

We understand the power of a smile. Even people we don't know make a positive impact on us through a smile. When someone we love smiles at us, the effect is dramatic. The smile of a parent or grandparent upon a child can often change that child's countenance and reaction to the circumstances around her. This facet of the family blessing is significant because it reinforces the high value God places upon His children and reveals the deep delight of His heart towards us in Christ.

Facet #3—God's Peace

The Lord turn his face toward you and give you peace...

He Gives His Full Attention

I was sitting across the table with a friend in a coffee shop talking about a significant event in my life. As I talked, my friend's eyes constantly darted around the room as other people came and left the shop. At one point in our 'conversation', his attention fixated on someone he knew coming through the door.

Our conversation was abruptly interrupted. He waved and signaled to this person to come to our table. We were introduced, and he was invited to join us. Our one-on-one conversation swiftly concluded. His attention switched from my unfinished story—and me—to someone else. I felt ignored and unimportant.

That isn't how it is with God. When God turns His face toward you, His full attention is directed to you. He is never distracted or diverted. As the Creator of the universe, He gives His full attention because He truly cares and wants you to know how much of a treasure you are to Him. His longing is to bless you by heaping His favor upon you.

Having said that, there is something that separates us from Him—the tragic reality of our sin. After the Fall, God had no choice but to turn His face away from all mankind. The glorious truth of the Gospel is that, through the cross, He has once again turned His face toward those who respond to His invitation to come under His umbrella of grace and receive His favor.

While His smile expresses His delight in us, His face turned or lifted towards us conveys His careful *attention* to us. That is truly amazing grace! His grace means His favor, and that means you have His full attention.

All the resources of heaven are at your disposal to accomplish His grand purposes through you. Among the resources available to those called by His Name is His peace—His Shalom. Shalom is the contented knowledge that God is seeking your highest good—your well-being. This is peace that transcends understanding. What could be a greater blessing!?

(See Appendix for some samples of general blessings other than Numbers 6.)

The Personal Blessing

The personal blessing represents another dimension of spoken blessing that differs from the general blessing in that it directs its attention to a specific person and circumstance. The personal blessing invokes a blessing intended only for that individual. It is similar to the patriarchal blessings with explicit messages of God's purposes for a specific child.

The blessing of the patriarchs communicated a prophetic anointing of God to carry forward the covenants of God through His chosen people. The personal blessing discussed here expresses a similar but distinctive purpose. Like the patriarchal blessing, it is a verbal confirmation of God's unique purposes attached to a specific individual unveiling itself through that individual's story.

Perhaps a description of some of the contexts for this type of blessing will help clarify. Here are two possible venues for speaking a personal blessing into the life of a child or grandchild. You'll also find some examples of these blessings in the Appendix.

Venue #1: Milestones

Milestones represent those once-in-a-lifetime events in life that warrant a special acknowledgment. Milestones are an opportunity to reinforce the special purpose God has in store for that person. They mark unique stages of an individual's life and how God is shaping that person for His purposes.

Diane and I were privileged to be at the hospital when each of our grandchildren were born. Our desire was to start them on their life journey with a blessing. We wrote out and framed a special blessing for each of them. We then spoke it over them in the presence of the parents before they left the hospital.

These were milestone moments in which we celebrated the beginning of a journey. We tried to use each grandchild's name as the milestone marker to emphasize his or her worth and the special purpose for which God made them.

Obviously, our grandchildren did not understand what we were doing at the time, but their parents did. They could not comprehend the meaning of the words we spoke. But because we wrote it out and framed it, each still hangs on their bedroom wall as a reminder of the amazing milestone moment when God reached down and touched him through us.

There have been other milestone blessings for our grandkids, including our times at GrandCamp each summer. These were special times to speak a blessing for each of our grandchildren to express the high value and special future we observed God unfolding in their lives. They always look forward to those moments, and still have copies of those hanging on the walls of their bedrooms too.

As you consider ways you can speak personal blessing specifically into the lives of each of your grandchildren (don't forget your adult children and spouses), here are some possible milestone "markers" that represent momentous opportunities for doing so:

- Milestone #1: Birth/Adoption
- Milestone #2: Starting School
- Milestone #3: Salvation and Baptism
- Milestone #4: Adolescent Transitions—Purity and Self-Control
- Milestone #5: Rites of Passage—Childhood to Adulthood (In the pattern of the Jewish Bar-Mitzvah or Bat-Mitzvah)
- Milestone #6: Graduation from High School, College, or Trade School
- Milestone #7: First Job or Career
- Milestone #8: Courtship and Marriage
- Milestone #9: First House
- Milestone #10: A Promotion
- Milestone #11: Major Accomplishment (book published, award, etc.)
- Milestone #12: Retirement/Change of Career

Venue #2: Blessable Moments

God gave Moses specific instructions for parents and grandparents to maximize several teachable, *blessable* moments. These are recorded in Deuteronomy 6:7 (NASB) – *"You shall teach them [God's commandments] diligently to your [children] and shall talk of them when you sit in your house and when you walk by the way and when you lie down and when you rise up."* These teachable moments can also blessable moments. They describe the natural, daily routines of life where opportunities present themselves to teach and speak blessing into young lives.

The point of this instruction from the Lord is to remind parents and grandparents of their responsibility to be intentional. A teachable moment is an opportunity to talk about life, God, and eternity. A *blessable* moment uses these same opportunities to also speak words of blessing at a very personal level. It's a timely opening for anointing your grandchildren with powerful words of high value and God's special favor.

Unfortunately, many American families miss these opportunities. A typical family today is filled with so much activity and distraction that these blessable moments are lost as we pass each other like ships in the fog. Grandparents, this is a perfect opportunity to fill the void. It doesn't matter whether you are a nearby or a long-distance grandparent. Geographical separation does not obviate the application of this command. It does, however, necessitate intentional, creative application. You can take advantage of blessable moments if you look for them.

Consider these typical *blessable moments* described in Deuteronomy 6:7-9 mentioned above:

1. When you <u>SIT IN YOUR HOUSE</u>

These are moments when family is gathered either formally or informally. It can be in the home or any place where you are together and have opportunity to come apart from the daily buzz of life to just sit and talk.

Mealtime is the most obvious 'sit-down' moment. But they are not the only ways families can sit together and enjoy *table talk*. Here are a few more opportunities to consider:

- Family game times, movie nights, or Wii tournaments: When your activity is over, why not sit down together and talk about what was enjoyed most and why? Conclude with a special blessing for each member of the family.
- A family reunion: Plan some sit-down moments in the schedule

to talk about family history, amusing stories, and lessons learned. Include a family blessing ceremony to wrap up the time together.

- Plan a time to go to a restaurant, movie, or other special event: Afterwards, grab a soda or ice-cream cone and talk about the experience. Look for a chance to affirm a quality you see in them in the form of a blessing.

- Telephone or email conversations: Speak or write a word of blessing. If no one answers a phone call, leave a message with a special blessing.

- Make some good use of the amazing internet tools available: Skype, or Face Time are great ways long-distance grandparents can experience a 'sit-down' moment with their grandchildren and adult children. Don't forget to end with a special word of blessing.

2. When you **<u>WALK BY THE WAY</u>**

Americans do not walk as much as previous generations. We much prefer driving, flying in an airplane, or using some form of public transportation. Most people would agree that Americans could use a few more walking activities. So now is a good time for us to make the effort to do more of it.

Here are a few *walk-along* opportunities that can be turned into blessable moments:

- Invite your grandkids to join you on a walk or hike. Keep your eyes open to the beauty of God's creation and turn it into a word of blessing. For example, you might say something like, "Look at the magnificent colors in the trees this fall. It reminds me of the beauty of God's handiwork when He made you. May God always fill you with the wonder of His handiwork in all of creation, including how wonderfully you are made!"

- When you witness an event or unusual situation as you're out and about, let it be a signal to stop and speak a word of blessing over someone along the path. Your example of doing something so out of the ordinary becomes a powerful example of living a life of blessing.

- A bike ride – affirming the wonderful way God has made them and given us the abilities to do things like riding bikes
- Walking through a museum or art gallery: Remembering that just as the artist made these art pieces, so God made you a unique masterpiece for more beautiful than any art man can create.

3. When you <u>LIE DOWN</u>

Bedtime is a wonderful time to talk about the events of the day, clear up issues, discuss some of life's lessons, and to pray together. It's also a grand time to speak the family blessing over a child.

You may not have regular bedtime opportunities as grandparents, but when you do get them, make them moments your grandkids will treasure, even as adults. At the end of a chaotic and activity-filled day, this is a great time to unwind with the grandkids and let them know how special they are. It will also help drive away certain fears they may have as young children. Here is an example of what you might say:

> _______, *may the Lord bless you and keep you in His loving and safe arms tonight. May you rest in peace knowing that He is with you and guarding you with His perfect love, and making His face shine upon you.*

4. When you <u>RISE UP</u>

How often is the mood of the whole day determined by the first few moments when everyone climbs out of bed? How you speak to your children and grandchildren in those moments can set the tone for everything that follows.

Unless you are raising your grandchildren or they are at your house for a sleepover, you may not have as many of these *rise-up moments* as parents do. There are, however, other ways you can engage *rise-up moments* with your grandchildren. Once again—it's all about intentionality. Here are a few practical ideas that may stimulate your thinking about a few of the *rise-up moments* we can enjoy as grandparents:

- Call once a week or once a month on a school day before they head off to school. Pray over them, speak a short blessing, and encourage them in their day.
- Make a blessing plaque to hang over their bed or on a mirror in their bathroom that they will see every day when they get up.
- For teenagers, send a text message each morning, or at least once a week, as they are heading off to school. Remind them how much they are valued and loved. It can be something as simple as, "May God bless you and keep you today. May the Lord fill you with the wonder of His creation and His special love for you. We love you, too. Nana and Papa."

In Tune with the Moment

Blessable moments are about spontaneous expressions. It is being in tune with the moment so that you can be a conduit of God's blessing for your grandchild—or some other person God brings into your life. I often will use words from the Aaronic blessing in Numbers 6:24-26 as a framework from which I speak. That is a good pattern, but it is more important that what you speak comes from the heart.

My daughter came by the house on her way out of town for a weekend tradeshow associated with her business. She needed a good income weekend to help pay off inventory expenses and bank a little extra. Before she left, I simply put my arm around her shoulder and said, "May the Lord bless you and keep you; may He prosper the work of your hands and pour out His favor upon you this weekend; may He be gracious to you and fill you with His peace." That's all I said.

They did have a good weekend; one of the best weekends of the entire year. I can't take any credit for that, and I don't know if what I spoke had any impact on the outcome. Speaking blessing is not a guarantee of financial success or any other desired outcome. Even so, do you suppose it might have reinforced God's goodness in my daughter's eyes?

Speaking words of blessing can be as simple as saying, "May the Lord bless you and keep you." Or it might reflect a special moment shared watching a spectacular sunset and saying, "As the beauty of this sunset displays the glory of God's handiwork, may the Lord make your life radiate the beauty of His glory in all you do."

God calls you to be His blessing-giver. Speak blessing often and speak it well. Live up to the role of blessing-giver. If you do, your children and grandchildren will be blessed, and they will call you blessed.

GRANDPAUSE...

THINKING IT THROUGH:

1. Consider the significance of each of the statements in the blessing of Numbers 6:24-26. How have you experienced those things from the Father? Do you think your children would be blessed to receive them from you?

2. Discuss the differences between the General blessing and the Personal blessing. Do you understand how to use each of these effectively? Talk about some ideas for using each of these in your family.

ACTION STEPS:

1. Develop a plan for implementing the practice of speaking blessing over your children and grandchildren using both the General and Personal (Milestone) blessings.

2. Pray for each other for wisdom and the courage to start a blessing tradition in your family and to share it with others in your church.

11

A Well-Versed Legacy

"The Christian is bred by the Word, and he must be fed by it."
–William Gurnall

Caroline is an heiress to a very great fortune. She describes the incalculable wealth her grandparents had amassed and left to her this way:

"From the time I was a little girl, my grandparents carefully chose their most valuable gemstones and gave them to me, one after another. It wasn't until years later that I realized they'd given me a priceless treasure. Today, I consider myself one of the richest women in the world. You can give your grandchildren the same inheritance. How?

The Psalmist said, 'The law from your mouth is more precious to me than thousands of pieces of silver and gold.' And in Proverbs we're told, 'Wisdom is more precious than rubies, and nothing you desire can compare with her.' My grandparents believed that. Their hearts were fully engraved with God's Word and they passionately passed it on."[1]

Could the legacy you are leaving your grandchildren be described as richly 'well-versed'? Nehemiah knew the importance of the Word. It was vital for the Israelites to remember who they were and how great is their God. It was God's Law that exposed their own sinfulness and led them to weep and repent. It was the Word that filled them with rejoicing as Nehemiah reminded them that the "joy of the Lord is your strength". Nehemiah and Ezra understood that the Word set them apart from the rest of the world and spoke words of life, hope and purpose.

Did you catch that the people stood from daybreak to noon listening to Ezra read the Law? That's six hours of non-stop Scripture reading! Wow! What a contrast from the typical sound-byte approach to Scripture reading we hear today in most churches or in our homes.

These men, women and children stood for six hours to hear God's Word. Why? They were hungry for the taste of truth. It probably also helped that their brains had not been programmed by visual and social media stimuli that reduces attention span. Nehemiah had laid a foundation for spiritual renewal among the people during the rebuilding, and now their hearts longed for a Word from God.

What place does the Word have in your family life? Is it taught, learned, memorized and lived in your life? The centrality of God's Word is what distinguishes true disciples from merely religious people. There is no greater treasure you can leave your grandchildren than God's Word hidden in their hearts. The Word will reveal the truth about God's love for them through Christ Jesus and keep them from sin. The Word combined with unshakable faith expressed through authentic worship opens the heart to the Gospel and the knowledge of God's grace for their salvation.

I love my work with the children in our church AWANA program. The mission of the program is to help children of all ages know Christ and serve Him unashamedly. Scripture memorization is the foundation of the program. While not all children are equally motivated to learn their verses each week, exposing them to Scripture and challenging them to memorize is planting seeds in their hearts for the rest of their lives, especially if someone in their family is participating with them and encouraging them to know and understand God's truth.

You may have grandchildren who are not particularly motivated to memorize Bible verses. I have one or two like that. Perhaps you have grandchildren as I do who have learning challenges. For them memorization of complex and abstract thought is extremely difficult. How do we help our grandchildren learn Bible verses if they fall into one of these categories? I'm not an expert, but here are some things I have found helpful.

Memorization Tips

I do some occasional work in theatre and church drama. I often hear people complain about having difficulty memorizing lines or lyrics to songs. I sometimes struggle with it myself. As a choir director for almost thirty years, I used to hear a litany of excuses why choir members could not memorize a single piece. Most people will tell you that they have poor memories or difficulty memorizing things. Obviously, this age of information inflation does stretch our memorization abilities and motivation. But is it the real culprit?

For much of human history, man depended upon memorization to transfer information from one person or generation to another. Before the printing press, few people had access to written documents or books they could read for themselves. They depended upon their memory to record what they heard so they could ponder it or pass it on to others. With all the printed materials available to us today and the technological mediums through which we gather information, memorization is not as valued in society as it once was. We do not exercise our minds as we ought.

Calculators and the internet, in fact, have contributed to diminished memory skills in America. We have become wholly dependent upon digital devices to store most our information. To be fair, there is far more information being dumped upon us today than at any other time in human history. It has been estimated that there is more information in one issue of a major metropolitan newspaper than a person would encounter in an entire year in the 1600's. Throw in email, the internet, blogs, e-books, smartphones and social networking, and you get some idea of the quantity of information bombarding our minds every day. With all this information so readily accessible, we seem to have much less need for recall and memorization.

Yet, despite the information overload we experience, we still memorize a great deal of information. For example, how many phone numbers have you memorized? I'll bet you know your social security number and perhaps your spouse's too. Think about other long numbers you've memorized such as bank accounts, addresses, safe combinations, or passwords (okay, maybe not passwords).

Most of us quickly memorize what is interesting and important to us. Vast amounts of facts and procedural steps are memorized by scientists, engineers, computer geeks, lawyers, doctors, accountants, politicians and law enforcement officers to name a few. Sports writers and commentators easily memorize large amounts of boring statistics about teams and individual players. The problem is not our inability to memorize. It is our motivation.

Some children are easily motivated to memorize Scripture with you. Most, however, will need a little coaxing. Your enthusiasm for the Word of God will help influence their eagerness to learn as well. Here are a few suggestions for cultivating a well-versed legacy with your grandchildren, some borrowed from Caroline Boykin's book, *The Well-Versed Family: Raising Kids of Faith Through (Do-Able!) Scripture Memory.*[2] She offers many excellent suggestions and proven tools for memorization.

Live Up to the Challenge

Let's be honest. We all need incentives for doing most things in life. Sure, there are many things we do just because they must be done whether we like it or not. You will not, however, find much success with your grandchildren by forcing them to memorize Scripture verses if they have no desire to do so.

I believe there is value in certain appropriate incentives as a means of helping our grandchildren memorize. Your primary objective is to help them to learn and hide God's Word in their hearts. There are several effective ways to motivate them to do that.

Having said that, there is the difference between providing incentive and bribery. Offering your grandson $100 to learn a few verses is bribery. Rewarding your grandchild with an outing to one of their favorite places after achieving a memorization goal is an appropriate use of incentive. Make sure you know the difference.

The goal is not merely Scripture memorization, but also a love for God's Word. The outcome we are seeking is to deposit God's Word in a child's heart where it may become a guide to truth and right choices throughout life.

Here are a few suggestions from Caroline's book and a few others that I believe will help cultivate enthusiasm for memorizing Bible verses:

- Select verses that are age appropriate. In most cases, you cannot expect a five-year-old to memorize long, complex verses that a teenager may struggle to learn. Even for older children, start out with short, simple verses that are easy to memorize.

- Discuss with them what the verses mean as they are learning them. Ask questions and share stories about how the verse or passage impacted your life.

- Make sure you are learning the verses with them. Don't expect them to enthusiastically learn Bible verses you are making no effort to memorize.

- Forget the verse references for younger children. When I worked with kindergarten, first grade and second grade children in our AWANA program. I tried to get them to learn the references with their verses. However, kindergarten and first graders have a great deal of difficulty with that. If I put too much emphasis on the book, chapter and verse number, they get distracted from the main objective of memorizing the verse. Some book names, like *Thessalonians,* are very hard for many young children to pronounce, much less memorize. As much as possible encourage them to learn the name of the book where the verse is found, but what is most important is to learn the verse and what it means.

- Develop creative approaches to make the learning and memorization something they look forward to doing. Use all your creative skills to find ways to motivate them to memorize. If you're baking cookies with the grandkids, or building a birdhouse, use the time to say verses together. Create some games and fun challenges as part of the learning process. You could turn it into a charades game and see if they can figure out what the verse is you are acting out.

- Develop fun and effective incentives for memorizing. You might set up a point system for each verse they learn. After so many points have been earned, they can use them to purchase items from Nana and Papa's General Store. Special outings, fun activities or craft projects could also be incentives for learning verses.

Write It Down

A well-versed legacy involves more than memorizing Bible verses. Clearly, that which authenticates and impresses God's Word into the hearts and minds of our children and grandchildren is an authentic life. Once we are gone, however, what will keep the legacy alive for the generations that follow? It will not be our pushing them to memorize, but how powerfully God's truth takes root in their hearts and how they live.

Writing down our stories and the lessons we have learned in life is another great way to preserve that well-versed legacy for other generations. The Bible provides some amazing stories of great men and women of faith from Abraham to Esther to Jesus and the Apostles.

Their stories, the stories of extra-biblical men and women of faith, and our own stories strengthen another generation's resolve to face the challenges of life with confidence in God's grace. Our story is important not only for today, but also for future generations who need to be well-versed in the history of God's faithfulness expressed through their own family tree.

My wife, Diane, started a process of creating a memory book of personal stories from her life to pass on to our daughters and grandchildren. She got the idea from a dear friend of ours, Lana Rockwell, who has written about how to pass on a written legacy.[3] Each year Diane adds new pages to the story book she started.

Our daughters consider it one of their cherished possessions. Besides providing meaningful insight into their mother's life, it also helps them understand how her story has shaped their own. Our stories are assets that need to be preserved so they can be handed down to the next generations as a source of blessing.

Other organizations like My Hope to You[4] offer tools and helps for providing a written record of your stories for future generations. We also have a digital download version of our former Legacy Journal[5] on our web site. It is another easy to use tool for leaving a written legacy. Whether something fancy, or something simple, these will be cherished reminders of a legacy worth outliving you.

The ball has been passed to you. It is in your court. How will you play?

GRANDPAUSE...

THINKING IT THROUGH:

1. What are the challenges you have with memorization? Has anything in this chapter changed your opinion about your ability to memorize?

2. How do you respond to some of the suggestions for encouraging your grandchildren to memorize Scripture? How do you think they will respond?

3. Discuss the section of this chapter that talked about leaving a written legacy. How valuable do you think it is to have a written record of our stories?

ACTION STEP:

Select one of the passages listed in this chapter and make it a matter of daily prayer over the next week asking God to show you how to be more intentional in matters of faith and spiritual growth with your grandchildren.

— 12 —

A Good Man's Inheritance

*"Those who give much without sacrifice are reckoned
as having given little."*
–Erwin Lutzer

You've seen them—the bumper stickers on the back of a large RV rolling along the highways that proclaim unabashedly, *We're Spending Our Kids' Inheritance!* Some think it humorous, though uncannily accurate… which makes it not so humorous, if you believe the wisdom of Proverbs 13:22: *"A good man leaves an inheritance for his children's children."* That's not the same message proclaimed on the bumper sticker. Maybe it's time to get a little perspective on the value of an inheritance.

Jim Stovall, author of *The Ultimate Gift*, tells the story of Red Steven's plan to help his wild and irresponsible nephew, Jason, learn the truth about the value of money. He wanted him to receive an inheritance that would be worth having.

Jason's Uncle Red died and left his will in the capable hands of his best friend and attorney, Theodore Hamilton. As executor of the will, Theodore Hamilton's job was to certify Jason's fulfillment of every stipulation of the will. These stipulations listed twelve tasks to be completed exactly as instructed, or there would be no inheritance.

Jason is given no information about what the inheritance is—only that Red refers to it as the 'ultimate gift.' He reluctantly agrees to do what his uncle asked, hoping to receive a large financial windfall in return. What Jason didn't expect was how the provisos placed upon him by his uncle would change him. Listen to what he says at the end of story…

> *"My Uncle Red's love for me in giving me the ultimate gift forever changed my life and who I am…and I am going to find a way to pass it on to deprived people who are as I was a year ago. I had no idea that the greatest gift anyone could be given is the awareness of all the gifts he or she already has. Now I know why God made me and put me on this earth. I understand the purpose for my life and how I can help other people find their purpose."*[1]

The journey on which Red sent his nephew ultimately set him free from his self-centered, entitlement view of life. He discovered that the real value of a full life has little to do with material wealth. He learned this because his uncle chose to give him something that money could not buy. It was a gift that would free him from the bondage of self and things. Red knew that if he didn't do it, probably no one else would. Jason was worth too much to let him destroy himself and others.

I wonder how well we learn the things Red did not learn till the end of his life—that giving those we love more *things* does not build character or help them experience Life (with a capital 'L') offered through the Gospel of Christ. The inheritance we pass to them can be a curse or a blessing. We hold the power of curse or blessing in our hands.

The purpose of an inheritance is not to be a supply line for all the worldly pleasures our kids and grandkids desire. Rather, it is serving as a conduit of God's grace and blessing from which real pleasures abound. If what we truly treasure is the material estate we build, it is likely our descendants will never learn the truth about possessions.

Selfish living is wasted living. You can help your grandchildren discover a better way. To do so, you must be willing to invest the time and effort to show them what really matters. If the things that do matter most are not the things that matter to you, you have little to offer them.

Imagine how their lives could change if they could see that the source of joy and delight in your life has little to do with worldly goods, but everything to do with your friendship with God. Seeing you make much of Christ as your all-satisfying delight may be the most significant illustration they will ever see of God's glory and greatness. If your life displays Christ as the one passion you cherish above all, is it not more probable they will be more inclined to want the same? It certainly increases the odds.

Of course, you can choose to waste your life by spending what you have on yourself. If that's the choice made, then the RV bumper sticker probably says it all. Not only will your life be wasted, but the investment opportunity of a lifetime will be lost as well. Is that the legacy you want to outlive you?

The greatest earthly asset or gift any grandparent can give their grandchildren is a three-letter word. It is YOU—your time, your values, your relationships, your faith and passion for Christ. A life that is rich toward God displays the splendor and goodness of God.

Not only does a good man's inheritance display the glory and greatness of God, it reveals the high value he places upon his children and grandchildren. He does not give them gifts without value, and certainly not those with harmful consequences.

What are your grandchildren worth to you? Does the inheritance you are preparing for them reflect that worth? I pray grandparents of my generation will choose to wisely invest all the resources entrusted to them for the next generation instead of throwing them away on useless things that ultimately burn up and bring no satisfaction.

Purses with Holes in Them

The Old Testament prophets are not particularly popular books to study these days. Yet, some of God's most important messages to His people, then and today, were spoken through these prophets. Consider, for example, the words of God through His prophet Haggai. He reprimands the people for putting so much effort and resources into building paneled houses for themselves while the house of God remained in shambles. *"Consider your ways,"* He warned. *"He who earns, earns wages to put into a purse with holes"* (Haggai 1:5-6 NASB). Sound familiar?

Enormous amounts of time and resources are invested in those of us over fifty building portfolios for ourselves while our families and the nation fall apart. It's time to pay attention to God's warning about giving careful thought to our ways.

Comforts and luxury rarely known at any other time in human history dominate our lives. Yet the pillars of truth and righteousness that give honor to our Creator and glorify Him who is the source of all blessings lie crumbled around us.

Today there are no lack of charlatans telling us that the blessing of God is found in things, pleasures, comforts, and safety. But beware—when that becomes our grid for evaluating God's blessing, we risk ushering in cursing rather than a blessing into our homes, churches, and businesses. We may not live the lavish life of a Bill Gates or a Mark Zuckerberg, but pleasure, beauty, wealth, power, and fame are still tempting treasures we to which we can easily fall prey. That's when the truth of God is exchanged for a lie.

Consider what we are reaping. Our ROI (return on investments) is measured by epidemic divorce and broken homes, narcissism, fluffy faith, miserly giving, and friendless friendships. Social, ethical, and moral responsibility has been sacrificed on the altar of folly and personal choice. Our grandchildren are forced to navigate a sea of uncertainty and existential hopelessness in a leaky rowboat with no paddle or compass to help them.

It's time for us to admit that our sought-after wealth has been stashed in *purses with holes in them.* We should not be shocked to see our own children and grandchildren seduced by this cursed delusion we helped birth. What is tolerated in one generation is deemed acceptable in the next, and finally fully embraced as normative in the third generation. Like the generations who came after Joshua's generation, we have chosen the path marked *Do-What-Is-Right-In-Our-Own-Eyes.*

Are you ready to implore God to search your heart, to repent for the foolishness there, and then ask, "Lord, what would You have me do now?"

In the 1970s, theologian and author Francis Schaeffer asked a similar question, which we failed to take seriously enough. He asked *How Should We Then Live?*[2] It is a question we dare not ignore any longer. A good place to start addressing that question is by considering how are we using the assets and resources God has entrusted to us.

Andrew Murray, South African pastor and writer in the early twentieth century, said this: "The world asks, 'What does a man own?' Christ asks, 'How does he use it?'" What are we doing to make sure the assets we have been given are being used to help turn the hearts of our children towards Christ and His righteousness?

Jim Elliott, martyred missionary to Ecuador, said it this way: "He is no fool who gives what he cannot keep to gain what he cannot lose." What does that look like in the context of who you are and what God has given to you? I'd like to suggest a new way of thinking about an old means of passing on an inheritance that might answer that question.

Not Your Ordinary Will

In some places in the world, living wills—a document authorizing someone we trust to carry out our wishes about the end of life—are common. A living will specifies the conditions under which we want to be *unplugged* from medical life support systems. I think it should be called a *death* will if its purpose is to tell others how we want to die under certain circumstances.

I'd like to suggest a different approach to the concept of a *living will.* Instead of thinking of it in terms of a death will as we normally do, let's create a living will that actually has to do with living—a LIVING living will. All right, I sense that deer-in-the-headlights look on your face. Stay with me. I think it will make sense.

Imagine creating such a will—an Ultimate Living Will, if you will--describing how we choose to remain *plugged in* to God's purposes while alive and active, rather than how we want to be unplugged. In other words, let's create a way of thinking about our assets that announces to those we love how God is directing us to invest those assets for Kingdom purposes while we're still living.

Jesus described it this way: being "rich towards God." Sound weird? It probably will be to a lot of people, but I think it more accurately represents the kind of Kingdom perspective by which Christians ought to live than the eat, drink and be merry angle.

This new *Ultimate Living* Will is a way to acknowledge in tangible ways that "life does not consist in an abundance of possessions" (Luke 12:15). Jesus talked so much about riches and how we view them. What I'm proposing is one way of assuming that heavenly perspective Jesus called His disciples to embrace.

It begins with an itemization of the assets God has given us, followed by a prayerful assessment of how God wants us to use all of them for His purposes. As His trustees and *workmanship*, how does He want these assets invested in a way that is "rich towards God".

The Ultimate Living Will bears witness to our families that the assets we have are really God's assets. It further expresses our desire to invest them, dispose of them, or distribute them so that others will know the joy, the delight, and the great amazement of living life in a way that makes much of Christ and the Father, rather than us.

When the funeral is over, our material possessions remain behind to be distributed to others, usually through a legal will or trust. We have no control over how those will be used. None of us will be around to oversee that process. It is possible that every material asset we leave behind will be wasted on worthless endeavors. The outcomes are out of our hands.

On the other hand, if millions of grandparents let the Gospel shape how they live and use what God has given them, imagine the impact of those lives on millions of other lives including their grandchildren. What would happen if Christian grandparents lived with such unshakeable faith that these words of Jesus were normal practice?: *"Do not store up for yourselves treasures on earth, where moth and rust destroy, and where thieves break in and steal. But store up for yourselves treasures in heaven, where moth and rust do not destroy, and where thieves do not break in and steal. For where your treasure is, there will your heart be also"* (Matthew 6:19-21).

Okay, enough of principles. What am I really talking about? How does the Ultimate Living Will actually work?

Material and Non-Material Assets

First, we need to recognize that God has given each of us both material and non-material assets. That's right—material and non-material assets. The traditional Will only deals with material assets. This new Ultimate Living Will paradigm is concerned with both. Non-material assets can have as much or more intrinsic value than any material asset in our estate. Non-material assets include things like family, friendship, faith, knowledge, education, skills, talents, spiritual gifts, wisdom from life experiences, time, and so forth.

The point is that while both material and nonmaterial assets can be invested, spent, or disposed of while we're alive, *non-material* assets will be forever gone when we die should we fail to use them as they were intended. Non-material, intangible assets can only be distributed by you—in the flesh. To unwisely hoard, hide, or carelessly waste these important assets, is to forever lose what was entrusted to us by our Creator to bless others.

The reality is that we can't risk waiting. We must do it now, while we still have breath and the ability to do it. Waiting till we die only guarantees two things. First, God's intended purpose for those personal endowments of our life will be diminished, if not lost entirely. We are the only ones who can employ those assets with all the meaning and power for which they were intended in those relationships.

Second, failing to invest what God has given us means we miss out on the joyful privilege and rich reward of being God's special conduit of blessing for those around us. What incredible blessing might be missed if we do nothing?

It is possible that God wants to supply something that only you and I can supply to someone in desperate need—perhaps in our own families? God delights in rewarding those who seek Him and obey Him. Why would we choose to lose the reward God wants to give by burying the gifts God has already given us to bless someone in a way no one else could do?

The *Ultimate* Living Will Principle involves three intentional actions:

1) Inventory your assets;
2) Prayerfully ask God to reveal how He wants these used now;
3) Set up a plan for distributing your material and non-material assets according to what God has revealed.

This simple, yet potent, approach to our possession (assets) can have a major impact on another generation as we display the joy and *glory* of what it looks like to live life created in Christ Jesus for God's glory. God's glory always involves the pouring out of is blessing on others as we open our hands for God to do more than we could imagine or think.

Yes, it takes courage to embrace such a radical idea. Most of all, it takes faith in what God's declares to be true—that being rich towards God is only way to live fully. In the world's eyes, it is pure foolishness. Courageous grandparents don't live to please men, but to live to the praise and glory of God so that they might be a conduit of blessing for another generation. The *Ultimate* Living Will is a but a tool that could do exactly that.

If you want to know more about building your own Ultimate Living Will, we have prepared a workbook by the same title to help you with this process. See the Appendix for information about this resource.

"When it comes time to die, make sure that all you have to do is die."
–Jim Elliott

GRANDPAUSE...

THINKING IT THROUGH:

1. What do you think the 'talents' of this passage represent for us today? Have you ever stopped to evaluate what your assets are?

2. How do you think the Master would respond to you if He returned today and demanded an accounting of how you have used the assets He entrusted to your care?

3. If you were to ask your family what they think is most important in your life based upon how you use all the assets God has given to you, what do you think they would say? What would your neighbors say?

4. We often think of "assets" in monetary or material terms. What are the nonmaterial assets God has also given you that demand equal attention and stewardship?

ACTION STEPS:

1. Make an inventory of all of your material and nonmaterial assets this week.

2. Ask God to show you how He wants you to use them to bless your children, your grandchildren, and others in your life.

3. Watch the film, *The Ultimate Gift*, together at some designated time, perhaps as a social event. Invite children and grandchildren to watch it with you and discuss.

PART FOUR

WISE UP!

Sanballat was very angry when he learned that we were rebuilding the wall. He flew into a rage and mocked the Jews, saying in front of his friends and the Samarian army officers, "What does this bunch of poor, feeble Jews think they are doing? Do they think they can build the wall in a day if they offer enough sacrifices? Look at those charred stones they are pulling out of the rubbish and using again!"

Tobiah the Ammonite, who was standing beside him, remarked, "That stone wall would collapse if even a fox walked along the top of it!"

Then the people of Judah began to complain that the workers were becoming tired. There was so much rubble to be moved that we could never get it done by ourselves....

Then as I looked over the situation, I called together the leaders and the people and said to them, "Don't be afraid of the enemy! Remember the Lord, who is great and glorious, and fight for your friends, your families, and your homes!"

When our enemies heard that we knew of their plans and that God had frustrated them, we all returned to our work on the wall.

–Excerpted from Nehemiah, Chapters 4 and 6 (NLT)

"Men of Issachar, who understood the times and knew what Israel should do..."
    –1 Chronicles 12:32a (NIV)

13

Modern Day Issachars

A people without understanding will come to ruin!
(Hosea 4:14)

I'm not an avid fisherman, though I do enjoy the thrill of wading into a fast-moving mountain stream with the sights and sounds of God's magnificent handiwork around me. Several years ago, my friend, Travis, decided I could use some instruction in the art of fly-fishing.

Though I still have a lot to learn, one thing Travis taught me that stuck was that successful fly-fishing (catching fish) involves much more than being able to cast well. He taught me it is equally important to understand what the fish are feeding on that day and in that location. Which is why he always stops by the local fly shop to talk with the resident guide about what the fish are biting that day. He knows the wrong fly will result in a disappointing day of catching fish.

King David may not have known anything about fly-fishing, but he did understand the importance of surrounding himself with knowledgeable men who give him useful advice. Scripture notes that the men of the tribe of Issachar were not only brave and skilled fighting men, but their distinctive asset was as *men who understood the times and knew what to do...* (1 Chronicles 12:32). These men provided a spirit of discernment that kept things in perspective in a time of uncertainty.

Such wise, clear thinking is as vital in our day as it was in David's. Our children and grandchildren need adults in their lives who have Issachar-like discernment. They need godly sages who see the world around them with spiritual eyes and know what to do. If wisdom is found among the aged, then it stands to reason that grandparents are positioned to be the modern-day equivalent of the men of Issachar for such a time as this.

When my oldest grandson was going through an especially difficult time in his life, another man suggested he needed to talk to someone in his family about the struggles he was having. He asked him if there was anyone he might be able to talk to about it. After some hesitation, he said, "Maybe… I might talk to Papa."

Thomas later told me that not more than two minutes after that conversation, he received a text message from me that said, "Thinking about you and wondering if there's a time we could get together and talk. I'd like to know how you're doing. Papa". That led to the first of several conversations together where he felt safe enough to talk about the hard things with me to help him navigate those rough waters.

We cannot afford to neglect the opportunity to create a safe place for a grandchild to talk through every day issues they face. Ignorance and abdication only give Satan an advantage in deceiving our grandchildren. We must not allow ourselves to be seduced by a pied piper's smooth-sounding tunes of self-centered pursuits that ultimately lead down a path of destruction. It's time to wake up and wise up to the responsibility we have to be an Issachar for the sake of our grandchildren.

Understand the Times

Amazing opportunities arise for those who choose to live intentionally, wisely and courageously as conduits of God's transformational power for another generation. But intentionality also demands we find out what the fish are biting. Otherwise, our effectiveness could be limited.

My prayer is that God will fill you *"with the knowledge of His will through all spiritual wisdom and understanding"* (Colossians 1:9). May that wisdom and understanding help you clearly see the world your grandchildren must navigate, a very different world from the one we knew as children. So, let's step out and seek some wisdom to understand these times, know what to do, and then have the courage to do it.

Culture 101

Let's begin by defining what we mean when we use the word *culture*. Here's a crash course in Culture 101 that I hope you will find useful. Andy Crouch uses the term *culture-making* in his book by the same title to describe how culture is changed or created. He suggests that we often misuse the word *culture* as a one-size-fits-all description of our society. In reality, society is made up of many cultures formed around geography, ethnicity, family structures and traditions, religion or faith, and specific *cultural goods* that characterize that culture.

In other words, no singular culture exists which describes every person or place in a specific country, city, or neighborhood. Any talk about American culture is actually a discussion about many cultures. While Crouch believes there is no such thing as '*the* Culture,' he argues, "finding our place in the world as culture-makers requires we pay attention to a culture's many dimensions."[1] So, how can we accurately understand it?

Culture is story. It is the story of man created in the image of God working to create his story in the context of God's larger story. Stated more simply, culture is what we make of the world, both in terms of what we do or create with what we have been given, and how we interpret and express the mystery, wonder and tragedies of our broken world. In other words, culture is shaped by our worldview—what we believe about who we are, where this world came from, and why we are here. Worldview is the accumulations of the assumptions and beliefs a person considers most important and by which he makes sense of the world. Thus, worldview impacts everything.

Isaac Newton, for example, completely reshaped the culture of the scientific world as a result of his work. But his work was the product of his worldview. He believed God was the Creator of a universe established and held together by natural laws. This led him to develop his theory of gravitation and three laws of motion. His work was the result of his observations of the wonder of God's design. He took what he observed, validated it, and compiled a new way of seeing our world and how it works that had never been suggested before. The Scientific Revolution occurred because one man, shaped by a biblical worldview, took what he had been given in this world and made something of it.

But what happens when a culture goes awry as it regularly does? Is it possible to transform it? Again, Crouch suggests that attempts to transform culture are largely misguided. He argues that we are not called to transform but to make or create a culture that replaces an existing one. Thus, while it is important to understand the culture or cultures in which we live, when it comes to changing it, we must first understand the culture God expects us to make in the first place. (By the way, Crouch also calls attention to the fact that family is the basic unit of culture— "culture at its smallest and most powerful." Strong families serve as a primary staging area for engaging culture and making something of it.)

Creating culture is the process of introducing something that the majority of society will embrace in exchange for what they already have. In other words, if culture is to change, something better will have to be offered that enough will want in exchange. Of course, that assumes there are enough who want something better. Either way, there are things that can get in the way of change. Let's look at a few.

Cultural Postures That Don't Work

Attempts at creating culture usually fail because of a faulty understanding about how culture is made. Crouch identifies three *postures* that actually hinder the process of changing, or more accurately, making culture. I have added a fourth. Any one of these alone can seriously obstruct any positive headway for re-making currently established cultural norms.

1. *Condemning culture*: My wife and I enjoy a steaming pot of ham

hocks with pinto beans served on cornbread on a cold winter day. It has been a tradition in my family for at least three generations. My grandkids, on the other hand, are not so crazy about beans and cornbread, even when it's smothered with ketchup (yummy!). However, no amount of sarcastic condemnation by the grandkids or our in-laws aimed at our beans and cornbread feast is going to change this cultural tradition as long as we're living.

If all we do is condemn a particular cultural tradition, we are not likely to produce a positive impact for change whatsoever. Rarely will anyone give up something unless something better is offered to take its place. Take television for example. We can sit around condemning the programs on television all we want, but the financial incentives of television producers are too strong to change what they do simply because a group of people condemn it. Unless a better alternative with equally viable economic benefits is offered, television programming will go on as it is—constantly deteriorating.

2. *Critiquing culture*: Crouch argues that a subtle approach to analysis and critique rarely affects culture. More education produces the same non-effect. Just because someone receives a carefully crafted analysis of all the fallacies and benefits of a thing doesn't mean that thing will change significantly. In fact, the likelihood it will produce long-term change is slim to none.

    My grandkids may serve up a nutritional analysis of our cornbread and beans with facts about how unhealthy it might be, but it won't change our tradition. Again, change can only be affected when something new and better is offered in its place, and so far, none of our grandkids have presented a better alternative to our cornbread and beans—at least, in my opinion.

3. *Copying culture*: In many western countries, attempts by Christians to create a Christian subculture with 'alternatives' to certain cultural goods has little impactd. Christian television networks surfaced in an

attempt to imitate the public market, hoping to offer a more palatable product. Both the music and film industry haven taken this approach.

Crouch argues that while these may be good for a particular subculture, they have no real impact on the prevailing public television, film or music culture. "Any cultural good, after all, only moves the horizons for the particular public who experience it," he observes. "For the rest of the world, it is as if that piece of culture, no matter how excellent or significant it may be, never existed… When we copy culture within our own private enclaves, the culture at large remains unchanged."[2] Copy-cat cultures have little impact on the rest of the world.

4. *Ignoring culture*: You've probably heard someone say, "Oh, just ignore it. It'll go away on its own." Culture may seem to morph or re-create itself over time, but it never does so without someone introducing the change. The surrounding cultures are formed by deliberate, intentional means by those who have the power to influence what is valued.

Sitting in silence only energizes another group of people to determine what cultural norms will dominate our society. Our grandkids can sit in silence and refuse to eat our cornbread and beans. However, it will still be served in our house because those of us who like it are in a position to keep it going. It will remain as a valued family ritual until another generation goes into the kitchen and creates a new cultural goods to take its place.

Understanding the culture around us is the first step towards impacting our world. But we will not understand the cultural influences that pervade our world if we do not also understand how worldview shapes those cultures. Our world is dominated by a secular worldview characterized by relativism.

A Postmodern Delusion

It is the best of times and the evilest of times—to reword a famous quote. This is not the only time in human history when evil has been called good and good evil. This has been the way of things since the Fall. John Piper comments that we should not "bemoan the disappearance of a lightly Christianized America. Rejoice that the Word of God has run and triumphed before (2 Thessalonians 3:1) in the very situation we find ourselves today."[3] When man attempts to explain and live a life apart from God, things quickly go from bad to worse. He lives in a delusion.

Postmodernism is a worldview that rejects the notion of a truth narrative for human existence. Absolute truth, for all practical purposes, is discarded in favor of individual choice which trumps everything, including God's moral law (moral law is utter nonsense in the minds of post-modern secularists). Thus, we have a society that is morally castigated and capable of egregious evil.

Relativism promotes the supremacy of individualism. In other words, truth is determined by an individual's feelings and level of comfort in coping with life. How that looks or feels can and does change daily. The societal cost of such thinking is enormous—community is devalued, tradition is debunked, ethics are ridiculed, and authority in scorned in favor of individual freedom. Self-restraint and self-sacrifice are rarely described as virtues. Self-actualization is the new virtue. Follow your heart, and trust it to show you the right thing. It is all that matters.

When the post-modern relativistic worldview prevails, moral standards are left to the whims of individual opinions, feelings and desires. Relativism propagates individual supremacy at enormous cost to society. Consider the consequences of a relativistic worldview in the current dominant view of marriage and family.

The Modern Family

Many television sitcoms, movies, and books satirize marriage as irrelevant and unnecessary. It is often portrays marriage as a limitaton in life than a liberating, fulfilling relationship in which family and society work together to find an anchor against the storms of life. This rapid demise of the traditional, historical understanding of both marriage and family is being fueled by three prevailing cultural norms (I call them 'abnormalities').

These abnormalities erode the essential foundations of a strong, stable society. We cannot afford to be silent on these issues. We have a responsibility to understand the messages they communicate and the consequences of embracing them. We must expose the lies for what they are working to restore a biblical view of marriage and family that challenges these abnormal views:

Abnormality #1: Divorce (*Reconstructing Marriage and Family*)
Divorce is the logical conclusion of the mindset that marriage is a *what's-in-it-for-me* proposition. Tim Keller, pastor and author of *The Meaning of Marriage*, suggests the eighteenth century Enlightenment circulated this view as it "privatized marriage, taking it out of the public sphere. During this period the purpose of marriage was redefined as individual gratification, not any 'broader goal' such as reflecting God's nature, producing character, or raising children."[4]

Obviously, there are circumstances in which divorce is unavoidable. However, when marriage is only a means to personal gratification and we combine it with no-fault divorce laws, the family suffers. The selfish interests of a husband and/or wife are quickly assigned more weight than the irreparable damage caused to the family and society.

Godly grandparents have both an opportunity and responsibility to tell the truth concerning the sanctity of marriage. They should also model it. I highly recommend a book by Josh Mulvihill, *Preparing Children for Marriage*[5], as a resource to help both parents and grandparents reconstruct a biblical view of marriage with your grandchildren that is healthy, enduring, and glorifies the One who instituted marriage.

Abnormality #2: Cohabitation *(Redefining Family)*

Though some research suggests that the divorce rate in the United States is back to what it was in the early 1960s, it's not all good news. The fact is that fewer couples are bothering to tie the knot, opting instead to live together.

According to a Pew Research study, cohabitation has skyrocketed since 1968. The study reports that the percentage of children living in a home where the adults live together, but are not married, has grown from 13% (9 million) in 1968 to 32% (24 million) in 2017.[6] Who knows what it is now. Many grandparents know too well the challenges these situations produce in their own families.

Most researchers admit every child needs a 'forever family'. They affirm that children benefit significantly when their biological mother and father are living in a committed marriage. Yet, they are amazingly silent about these things in the public square.

Grandparents ought to be on the front lines battling for biblical marriage and family as God designed it. We cannot allow the enemy to steal this gift God instituted for the common good of spouses, children, extended family, and society as a whole. We must talk about what marriage really is and model it in our homes. It is imperative that the whole truth about marriage is told--the amazing blessing marriage can be for those who enter it according to God's design, and the dangers of distorting that design.

Abnormality #3: Same-Sex Marriage *(Redefining Marriage)*

Now an assumed norm, most Western nations have adopted laws legalizing same-sex marriages. Some laws impose severe fines, and even imprisonment, for daring to suggest same-sex marriages are wrong.

Many argue we are making a mountain out of a mole hill. Let same-sex couples marry. What difference does it make? Besides, it's inevitable, so why make a big deal of it? But it is a big deal—one that impacts the honor and sanctity of marriage as instituted by God. In other words, what God says about marriage matters.

This is not a comfortable topic for many Christians. We know we will be labeled bigots because of our beliefs about marriage. But such intimidation must not keep us from talking about it. Parents and grandparents must not be forced into a *spiral of silence*[7] on those issues that matter to God and impact the future of our families. We live in a time when the trend is to cower in silence as those in power bully their way into public thought and policy.

Before we go mouthing off in the public square, we better be sure we understand what God, who is our Creator, says about marriage. If we are to teach and speak to it intelligently and compassionately, we need to be informed. At the same time, there will be reprisals from those who do not want the truth taught.

Make sure you know what the Word of God teaches so you will recognize the counterfeits. Let God's Word speak for itself. The Bible is clear about God's definition of marriage as a unique relationship and sacred institution established by Him **between a man and woman**. Do you care what God says and that anything else is a lie?

There is an unabashed attempt to abolish all historic meaning from this sacred institution. Adam Mersereau correctly assessed the motive behind the same-sex LGBTQ movement when he wrote, "Gay activists claim to believe marriage is so meaningful that it should be extended to gays, but their case rests upon the belief that marriage is so meaningless that it can be claimed by anyone who wants it."[8] We have yet to see to full implication of this belief.

There are a few in the gay community who do not support same-sex marriage and pay the price for saying so. Doug Mainwaring is one of them. He paid dearly for his opinion published in an article for Public Discourse explaining why he believes same-sex marriage should be opposed.

> *"The notion of same-sex marriage is implausible, yet political*
> *correctness has made stating the obvious a risky business.*
> *Genderless marriage is not marriage at all. It is something else*
> *entirely… To give kids two moms or two dads is to withhold from*

them someone whom they desperately need and deserve in order to be whole and happy. It is to permanently etch 'deprivation' on their hearts."[9]

Doug is right, and he argues not from the point of view of faith or 'religion', but common sense. He acknowledges that there are those who delight in "slowly chipping away at the bedrock of American culture: faith and family life." This is not relevant only to American culture. The consequences of eroding that bedrock extend well beyond America. Are you willing to have this conversation with your grandchildren?

The position we take on this issue must be expressed with both truth and compassion. If we are to engage in honest dialogue with our grandchildren's generation, they must know we care about them as much as we care about the truth. Learn, ask questions, and know what you're talking about. Understanding, coupled with genuine love and compassion, can open amazing opportunities for dialogue and discourse, especially in your own family. Many young people have simply never been offered an alternative view.

My daughter shared a conversation she had with an eighteen-year-old girl who grew up in a good home. Her family did not talk much about faith or the Bible. As the two of them discussed views on same-sex marriage, my daughter shared a few things the Bible had to say about marriage. Her response was, "I've never heard that before. No one ever told me there was another point of view." If you don't talk about it, it is likely no one else will either. And it's never too early to start the conversation.

Traditional marriage, in which there is a committed father and mother, is and always will be God's sacred means for creating, nurturing, protecting, and educating children. Divorce, co-habitation and same-sex marriage all stain what God calls sacred. If it is important to God, it ought to be important to us.

More Casualties of Relativism

At the end of the day, the frivolous pursuit of happiness apart from God ends up impaled upon the sword of despair. Proverbs 16:25 says, *"There is a way that seems right to man, but in the end it leads to death."* The same self-centered views of relativism that impact morality and family relationships also impact other areas of life.

Here are two other casualties of a post-modern relativism worldview I urge you to explore further.

1. Devalued Life

A worldview that says, "Do what is right in your own eyes", dramatically impacts the value we assign human life. Devoid of a biblical worldview that celebrates the Imago Dei stamped upon every human soul at conception, a worldview built around personal choice soon overrides all concerns about the dignity and sanctity of human life.

Darwinism, the crown jewel of postmodern philosophy, is diametrically opposed to the notion of a Creator and a purposeful creation. When life has no meaning or purpose, neither does it have any value. It's not hard to imagine the consequences of such a worldview if we stop long enough to think about it—abortion, human trafficking, slavery, assisted suicide, euthanasia, and rampant violence.

The outcome of a Darwinian worldview is to assign the value of human life purely on utilitarian terms. Whether we are talking about persons who are handicapped, the mentally impaired, or the elderly who can no longer care for themselves, the dignity and sanctity of all life is at the heart of the Gospel. The Gospel is built upon the foundation that man is created in the image of his Creator, and in that truth is the value and worth of human life, not physical or mental capacities. No other creature is made in God's image.

2. Designer Religion

Writing for *USA Today,* Cathy Lynn Grossman, quotes George Barna: "We are a designer society. We want everything customized to our personal needs—our clothing, our food, our education. Now it's our religion."[10] At the smorgasbord of relativism, you can pick whatever makes sense to you:

"I'll have a little belief in God—as long as it suits me. Some
Bible will be fine, but only the tasty portions, if you please. And
I'll take some grace, but leave off the repentance, please. Oh, let's
see, I'll have a little Jesus with some Eastern mysticism thrown in
for dessert."

Speaking the truth is not popular. Truth is often unpleasant, and it may seem offensive to some, but it is also life-giving. Jesus promised the truth would set us free. Grandparents, we must not surrender our place at the city gates of our families where we are to serve as gatekeepers of truth for the next generations. As our children wander through the darkness of relativism and deception, our homes ought to be a place where the light is always on, so they can find their way.

We can't pick and choose what we want to believe. God is the standard for truth, not man. Today, topics about sin, repentance, obedience, and self-denial are often avoided in favor of large doses of grace, forgiveness, happiness, and love. Look, I cherish these sacred truths dearly, but not as a tool to make people feel good at the expense of their souls. When the heart of the Gospel is missing, it is stripped of its full meaning and transformational power.

There is another major component of today's world for which we need wisdom and understanding—technology. How does the Gospel shape how we use technology? We'll explore this complex and imposing reality in the next chapter.

GRANDPAUSE...

THINKING IT THROUGH:

1. What is culture? Why do you think Christians have much impact upon the culture in which they live? How can grandparents make an impact in culture?

2. What does worldview mean and why it is important?

3. Describe your understanding of the postmodern (secular) worldview expressed by relativism. How does relativism line up with Romans 1:18-32? Read Proverbs 16:25. How does this speak to the problem of relativism?

4. What is the difference between a multi-generational and inter-generational point of view? How can we counter the negative effects of individualism and generational separatism in our day and in our culture?

5. What are ways we can begin to create opportunities for dialogue with our grandchildren and others that would help us understand the world in which they live?

ACTION STEP:

Take some time to examine your own worldview this week. Does it line up more with culture or Scripture? I urge you to get a copy of ***The Story of Reality*** by Gregory Koukl to help you understand how your worldview lines up with the Bible.

14

Tech-Wise Grandparenting

"The biggest cultural mistake we can indulge in is to yearn for technological solutions to our deepest cultural problems."
–Andy Crouch

Tom and Betty looked forward to celebrating Thanksgiving with their daughter and family now living 2000 miles away. They pulled out all the stops for this overdue reunion. Knowing they had but a few precious days to enjoy their family, Tom and Betty did not want to waste a single moment. They decided that the computer, TV, and cell phones would be turned off to minimize disruptions in their few treasured days together.

When the much-anticipated reunion took place, it was nothing short of joyous. A torrent of unrestrained hugs and kisses hailed their arrival. No sooner had the last hug ended and coats were hung, then their cherished reunion was interrupted by a cacophony of beeps, dings, and obnoxious ring tones.

The dinner table was no different. The grandkids continued to send and receive text messages with their friends. One came to the table with his iPod earphones stuffed in his ears, tuned out to any conversations that might occur. Apparently, daughter and family never received the memo highlighting Tom and Betty's plan for a distraction-free visit.

Sound familiar?

I suspect you know something about the unwanted digital visitors intruding upon family gatherings, am I right? This intruder robs us of meaningful personal exchanges with our loved ones and leaves us feeling relationally disconnected. Our digital devices have a way of unexpectedly wreaking havoc on family interactions. The Norman Rockwell rendering of a family joyfully sharing life around the table does not reflect the reality of most families today.

Where families once lived and worked side by side on the family farm, each sharing common tasks drawing them into a tight-knit community, technology has now segregated into individual cocoons. In our digital world, both personal and work life are entangled in endless links to outsiders via smartphones, email, Instant Messaging, and social media. These technological wonders also possess an uncanny ability to impede relationship bonding and enjoying shared experiences. In their place is the relentless invasion of virtual 'friendships' and out-of-control conversations.

Christine Rosen, senior editor of *The New Atlantis*, believes the constant virtual connections created by technology directly disrupt shared endeavors. She explains, "What family members do around each other at home has less and less to do with each other... Every public space is now potentially a scene for the private if we can reach out to those we know via technology."[1] How are we to respond to this technological intrusion upon personal relationships, especially in our families?

Everything about life is dramatically impacted by technology, particularly media technologies. High definition television, computers, DVRs, iPods, iPads, e-books, smartwatches and smartphones are as commonplace in our world as roads and highways. With the exception of television and a few personal computers, most of these technologies did not exist or were not available to the general public before 1990. These new technological highways have changed the landscape of our lives. For many of us who are grandparents, it's as exasperating as a mosquito in a mannequin factory.

Grandparents, who would have imagined that in our lifetime, nearly every person on the planet would carry a cell phone or smartphone connecting him or her to almost anyone in the world? In 1960 it would have been inconceivable that everyone would someday have his or her own personal computer—let alone multiple computers in various sizes and shapes? Few of us envisioned devices called smartphones, smartwatches, iPads or notebooks that would allow us to carry our personal computer on our wrist or in our pocket. Cars that park themselves with hands-free steering or drive themselves were things only imagined in sci-fi films and comic books.

We certainly are not in Kansas anymore—or even Oz. Our world is now a technologically dependent world. Things will never be the same. Who knows what new technologies will emerge to change the landscape again in the next few years? Welcome to the age of technology. We would be foolish to ignore it. The wise will learn and understand the realities and dangers behind this technological age.

Tech-Dummy to Tech-Savvy

Courageous, gospel-shaped grandparents know technology is here to stay, but they care about minimizing the polluting effects of technology in our lives. Left unchecked and uncontrolled, we understand the havoc technology can inflict upon our grandchildren and our world.

Right now, you may wonder if anything can be done other than sit back and watch it happen. It's overwhelming. Technology seems to have a life of its own. Sometimes it feels like we're on a runaway train with no engineer heading for a huge canyon, and the bridge is out. How do we stop the train?

Perhaps you are one of the few people who don't really care. You resist having anything to do with the new technologies. You don't give a hoot about computers, email, or Skype. If you have a cell phone, you prefer a 'dumb' phone over a 'smart' phone. You want no part of Facebook or Twitter and see no reason to learn how to text. You don't know an app from a tweet and don't want to know. You have *tech-apathy* and are content to be a *tech-dummy*.

On the other hand, if you are a typical grandparent age sixty-five or younger, you probably have several of the latest tech-gadgets. You keep in touch with your grandchildren through email, texting, and Skype (or

Facetime). You are actively connected on Facebook and Twitter. You are proud to be as tech-savvy as you are. The question is… are you *tech-wise*? Do you understand the dangers of the technology you have embraced?

You may be that grandparent who falls somewhere in between, not quite sure how much technology you should embrace, and wary about getting caught up in the technological frenzy. You are tech-wary because you are tech-aware. You recognize the dangers and are concerned about how much is too much.

Wherever you are in the spectrum of technological comprehension, personal use, or level of comfort, I recommend every effort be made to know something about what is going on, even if you aren't going to use it. Disciplined discernment is essential. If you want to help your children and grandchildren use it well, you'd better know something about the beast prowling the land.

Before you roll your eyes and put down the book, I ask you to read on and not give up yet. You don't have to be a geek to figure out a technological game plan.

Grandparenting in a Digital World

Many of us old geezers are fond of proclaiming how well we got along without any of this new technology. We're good about complaining and criticizing the new-fangled gadgets we don't understand. Whether you are tech-savvy or not, I'll bet your grandchildren are. If the only thing they hear from you is complaints and tirades about the evils of technology, the opportunity for meaningful dialogue will likely shut down.

On the other hand, an expressed willingness to engage their world and attempt to understand it will earn you a voice in their world at some point. So, before you rush out and enroll in a computer class or sign up for a course on some of the newest technologies, here are a few principles for building a technological foundation:

1. **God is the creator of technology**. He created our brains and all the elements and laws of nature that allow technology to work the way it does. Made in God's image, we are creators by nature, made to create and be creative. Technology is a logical result of man's creativity and God's creative genius in the things He has made. So, whether we are talking about cars or computers, heating pads or iPads, technology exists because God created a world where man has unimaginable possibilities for expressing his creativity.

2. **Technology is not inherently evil or sinful—we are**. But neither is it neutral. Technology can be used for good or evil, because like the rest of creation, it is also cursed. If there are abuses and wrongful uses, it is because we are by nature sinners prone to use good for evil.

   Unfortunately, too many well-meaning Christians are quick to pounce on new technologies and denounce them as inherently evil. Television, movies, the internet are examples of technologies that have been condemned as evil. Technological creations are not by nature evil, but because we live under the curse, they can be instruments through which evil and corrupt purposes gain a foothold.

   The same was true for the printing press. Shall we throw out all books as evil and sinful because there are authors who use them for such purposes? How about the light bulb, or the typewriter...or curling irons? Where shall we draw the line between what is good and what is not? Attempts to do that often result in even more evil.

   Technology is not neutral despite it being an inanimate, soul-less thing. Like so many other inanimate objects, it too can easily become an idol. How we use it and how we view it determine whether it becomes an instrument for good and the glory of our Creator, or an addictive means of harm and destruction. All the dangers of technology that we will explore are rooted in the sin nature.

3. **Technology can be used for good**. There are plenty of good uses for the technologies men create. We must pay attention to the dangers, but if that is all we do, we will miss the possibilities for making use of these things as instruments of good. Dr. David Murray, Professor of Practical Theology at Puritan Reformed Theological Seminary, produced a helpful video to teach children *disciplined discernment* in the proper use of technology for the glory of God and for their own good.[2] Our goal should be to help them avoid the pitfalls of technology and to make wise choices in the use of it.

The Lure of Digital Idolatry

The constant flow of new technology and its applications prey upon our greed and the need to keep up with the Joneses. We are besieged with messages leading us to believe the latest technologies are must-have items. Fear of becoming obsolete fuels our obsession with the continual barrage of deceptive marketing schemes luring us to the latest tools (toys) so our lives will be easier and better. Apple has mastered the marketing message as well as anyone.

We've bought into the lie we must have it now. People stand in long lines the night before the release of the newest version of the latest iPad or iPhone so they will be one of the first to have it. Once they have it, they are consumed by it and the need to continually upgrade for more speed, a larger selection of apps, and more features.

Other technologies such as Xbox video game systems, tablets, YouTube, Apps and social network sites consume young and old alike. Greed and the lust for more dictate our impulsive buying habits and consuming addictions. We are easily lured into making technology our god. Only disciplined discernment rooted in God's truth and virtue will keep us from being caught in the deceptive web of 21st century technologies.

Disciplined discernment is the *understanding-the-times* portion of the Issachar Factor. Do you remember Tom and Betty in our previous chapter?

How would you handle that situation? Would you write it off as not important enough to make it an issue, or would you take a stand?

Disciplined discernment is not being annoyed over something you don't understand. It is not burying your head in the sand and pretending it doesn't matter. Discernment is the ability to identify the real danger—in this case, the addictive nature of unfettered accessibility to devices that can lead to the destruction of meaningful community and genuine relational intimacy.

The loss of relational intimacy and accountability produces unhealthy and dysfunctional families. It disconnects and undermines personal relationships that are so crucial to maturity and purpose. Our technologies are poised to become a new form of idolatry keen to control us if we are not careful and wise.

Smartphone Wisdom

There is no time to examine all the technologies of our day in a book like this. But one technology we need to address is especially powerful and dominant throughout the world—the smartphone and its new cousin, the smartwatch. This is a technology as common as an automobile, but without the age restrictions. Your grandchildren use it as though it were an extra appendage.

Here are some due diligence principles for grandparents who want to be effective change agents in their grandchildren's lives.

Four essential considerations every grandparent should keep in mind when talking to your grandchildren about smartphones:

1. **You are not their parents.** As such, you do not have final say-so. But you can have a powerful influence in their thinking as long as it's not at the expense of the parents' authority.

2. **You can't help them understand what you do not understand.** Do you understand what a smartphone is for and why it needs to be redeemed if it is to be used for good? Since the Garden the whole problem with the human heart has been trying to build our identity

around something besides God. When we put anything (including our devices) in the place God and His desire for our best, it will disappoint and destroy us… and others.

It is a sad fact that many children and youth frame their identity around a smartphone? Ask them if that is a good thing. Tech devices also fall under the power of the curse. Smartphones can be used for good, but also for evil. Do you understand what a smartphone is for? What is its purpose? When does it step beyond that purpose? Let me see if I can help you with that.

Your grandchildren may be tempted to think of their smartphone as their access to anything they want. And they would be right. However, your job is to guide them to understand that access without wisdom is highly dangerous. Explore with them the realities of smartphones (pornography, sexting, sneaky apps, fake social media accounts, etc.) that become deadly lures and traps if we are not on guard. If smartphones were all good, why would they need 'sneaky apps'? If they feel the need to hide something, why would anyone imagine what is being hid is something good?

Talk about how their smartphone could be a way to use their skill and wisdom to apply knowledge to a specific goal—like helping others or researching a school project. The purpose of a smartphone is not unrestricted access to anything that may come along, or texting non-stop, but the ability to wisely access that which is useful, profitable, excellent, praiseworthy and noble.

3. **Guide them from a position of trust.** Do they know that you are a safe place for them to talk about things like this? Have you said to them, "You can tell me anything and you can trust that I will be fair. I won't overreact because I love you"?

4. **Set the example on using a smartphone.** Do you practice what you preach? Smartphones are almost as bad in the hands of older adults as they are with kids. Is your smartphone (assuming you have one) a

constant appendage on the end of your arm as well? If you talk and text at the dinner table, you can hardly expect them to not do it.

If your anxiety level goes up dramatically when you can't find your phone or when you leave it at home, you might want to re-examine your own unhealthy attachment to it.

Smartphones have given us so many options, many of them good. I am so glad that I have GPS on my smartphone when I don't know how to get somewhere. I love having a camera and a built-in flashlight when they're needed. I am grateful for having a mobile boarding pass on my phone when I can find my paper one.

They also have many not so favorable realities that can make us unwisely dependent upon them, often for things we don't really need. Most of all, they can hinder relationships, or having a conversation with a stranger in the airport (ever notice how almost everybody is on a cell phone?). Sometimes less is more.

Getting More Out of Less

Understanding the problem is a good beginning. Sadly, many parents do little to help their kids 'get it', perhaps because they don't get it either. Children are often left to figure out life and relationships on their own with technology as their mentor. Grandparents, let's not make the same mistake.

Here are a few suggestions you can use to help focus on relationships by using less technology and more personal interaction times. I call these Tech-Free Zones and Recesses:

1. Family Gatherings: Set up rules where family members turn off all cell phones, iPods, and other electronic devices when they come to your home for a family event. You can provide for emergency contact needs by assigning one cell phone that responsibility (preferably an adult).

I created a cell phone caddy I place by the front door when we are expecting family and guests for a long period of time. On it is a short poem I wrote asking our visitors to deposit their phones. It reads:

> As family, friend or special guest,
> We want our time to be the best;
> So, thank you for this one request
> To silence your phone and give it a rest!

2. Grandkid Visits: When the grandkids come to visit you, help them understand the value of hands-on relationships by establishing tech-free zones or recess periods during their visit. For example, tech-free zones ought to include the family table, bedrooms and other designated areas you choose. Tech-free recesses are agreed upon periods of time in which all devices are put away, and you engage with them in pre-planned activities (baking cookies, doing a puzzle, reading a book, sharing stories, etc.).

3. Special Outings: Plan a special outing with your grandchildren ten years of age and older. This works well if you can take them one at a time, but a group outing works too. Plan it around an event or activity they can enjoy, but no movies or electronic game arcades allowed. Take them to a local museum, the zoo, a theme park, a theatrical play, or plan a picnic, a hike, a trip to the beach, or an excursion in the mountains. The possibilities are limited only by your imagination, location and physical abilities.

    Whatever you do, one requirement is that cell phones or other electronic devices are left at home (you can keep one for emergencies). The objective is to have fun and to engage in meaningful conversation (which can be fun too). Parents may be included in the outing, but something powerful happens when it's just you and your grandchild.

While spontaneity is good, you might want to think ahead about a few questions you can talk about when you are together. For example:

- *Who is your best friend?*
- *What do you most like about this friend?*
- *What do you think it means to be a friend?*
- *Besides TV or video games, what thing do you most enjoy doing?*
- *Why do you think God made you and put you here?*

Make sure you listen a lot. Encourage them to talk. If you share one of your stories, don't dominate the conversation talking about you, and make sure you are transparent, honest, and relevant to the topic being discussed.

4. Instead of a tech-free outing, plan a fun-filled tech-free adventure with your grandkids. Let them know ahead of time that they will not be using any modern technology devices like TV, computers, Xbox, Game Boys, cell phones, iPods, iPads, microwaves, or radios. Explain that everyone will pretend they are pioneers. (If you know someone who owns a farm or ranch, this can be even more fun.) Create a whole day of activities that require you to work together and discover the wonders of life that can be experienced without technology.

This isn't rocket science stuff, but it can be powerful moments that your grandchildren rarely get to experience. These will be memories and relationships they will remember well into their adult years. Don't be hindered from doing them because you think your grandkids won't like it. They may not, but it's worth the risk to find out, don't you think?

Now that we understand a little more about being 'tech-wise', let's apply some of this wisdom to a few other potential traps in this technological age for which we need to apply wise due diligence.

GRANDPAUSE...

THINKING IT THROUGH:

1. Do you agree with the three principles of technology? Why or why not?

2. In what ways has technology become a source of idolatry today? Can you cite any examples in your own life, family or friendships that illustrate this?

3. What are your feelings about today's technology? How are you dealing with the smartphone issue? Is your attitude providing a good example or causing some level of alienation for your grandchildren?

ACTION STEPS:

1. Make the decision to intentionally learn what you can about today's technologies (you don't need to be an expert). Determine to read one or more of the technology resources listed in Appendix 1. Pick one or two that could help you become more knowledgeable on this subject and give you more opportunities to talk with your grandchildren without appearing out of touch.

2. Pick one Tech-Free activity you could do with your grandchildren. Build a plan, set a time and put it into action. Share with some others how it went and what you learned.

15

Avoiding Technology Traps

"Our imaginations are what help us change the world."
–Shane Hipps, author of *Flickering Pixels*

As image-bearers of our Creator, we have been blessed with the ability to imagine and create. Those same gifts can also turn into a curse. Technology reveals both the amazing ability God has given man, and the tragic consequences of using those gifts for anything other than the glory of the One who made us in His image.

Technology provides limitless circuits in which to explore. Wisdom tells us that certain decisions direct us onto a specific life path. Every path we choose has a pre-determined destination—life or death. Those are the only two options. This is why the Bible says, *"Trust in the Lord with all your heart and lean not on your own understanding; in all your ways acknowledge Him, and He will make your paths straight [direct your paths]"* (Proverbs 3:5-6).

The digital world is fraught with treacherously dangerous pathways filled with traps the Enemy uses to prey on our weaknesses. Wisdom is required to understand these for what they are. It is tempting for grandparents to look the other way and not say much. After all… Mom and Dad are responsible, right?

We are especially susceptible to this destructive attitude if our motive is to keep peace in the family. We want our grandkids to like us, so keep your mouth shut! It might be tempting to ignore the issues, but that would be a mistake. Why? Because technology plays a huge role in what's at stake for our grandchildren souls.

We can tell ourselves it's not our responsibility. That's a cop out. God designed the family as a partnership between parents and grandparents to train up a child. When that partnership is working in harmony, something powerful is unleashed in us to help our grandchildren avoid these dangerous traps.

I have selected four major technology traps I believe need our diligent attention. If we ignore these, our grandchildren could pay the price.

TRAP #1: Death by Amusement

Author Neil Postman wrote long before digital technology arrived on the scene that the real threat to society would not be a Big Brother oppressor, but people who choose to "adore the technologies that undo their capacities to think."[1] He analyzed our word 'amuse', who's root is the word *muse*. Muse means 'to think'. The negative prefix 'a' added to 'muse' negates the original meaning. Thus, *amuse* means 'not to think'.

The amusement assault through technology sedates us so that mental focus on important issues and matters of life becomes difficult to attain. The ability to fix one's attention enough to think critically and sensibly is as rare as a politician keeping a campaign promise. Sound bites and rapid-fire commentaries diminish our ability to ponder and assess the substantive issues of life. Social media exposes our diminished capacities to evaluate what is true and to act with civility.

Amusement in the form of entertainment drives much of today's technology. The addictive propensity of entertainment can consume most of our waking hours before we know it. Immersed in entertainment via TV, Xbox and gaming, texting, Facebook, and internet apps, little time is available for those things which build character and develop imagination. What a child repeatedly sees and hears determines…

- What that child will retain,
- How that child will think or not think, and
- What values he will embrace. Sesame Street taught children to love

school, but the unintended consequence is that children love school only if it is entertaining like Sesame Street.

According to a 2010 article in the *New York Times*, the more a child is bombarded with the various media stimuli of our culture, the more their brains are literally rewired to think in illogical and disconnected thought patterns. The fallout of this means they are "more habituated…to constantly switching tasks—and less able to sustain attention."[2]

That's because extensive media exposure rewires brain activity to the right side where incoming messages are not analyzed by logic, but by emotion. Emotion is the essence of entertainment. The result: Children (and adults) are programmed to depend on feelings rather than critical thinking and assessment to influence how they respond. By contrast, the brain of a child who reads a great deal, or is read to frequently, develops a strong ability to think logically and critically—a left-side function.

It's not hard to connect the dots when it comes to matters of faith and truth. When confronted with the explosion of ideas and unfiltered opinions that continually pass through the digital network, the inability to think critically will lead to immature and unstable emotional reactions without substance or basis. James says such a person is like the *"wave of the sea, blown and tossed by the wind…he is a double-minded man, unstable in all he does"* (James 1:6, 8).

Contrasting two popular works by George Orwell (1984), and Andrew Huxley (Brave New World), author Neil Postman made this profound observation:

> *"Orwell feared those who would deprive us of information.*
> *Huxley feared those who would give us so much that we would*
> *be reduced to passivity and egoism. Orwell feared that the truth*
> *would be concealed from us. Huxley feared the truth would be*
> *drowned in a sea of irrelevance. Orwell feared we would become*
> *a captive culture. Huxley feared we would become a trivial*

culture, preoccupied with some equivalent of the feelies, the orgy porgy, and the centrifugal bumblepuppy…In short, Orwell feared that what we hate will ruin us. Huxley feared that what we love will ruin us."[3]

May God give you and me His spirit of wisdom and understanding to hate evil and love the truth, and to know how to teach our children and grandchildren to do the same.

Taking the 'A' Out of Amusement

What can we do to keep our grandchild's mind engaged? Here are a few suggestions.

- Make time for reading to and with your grandchildren rather than allowing them to sit in front of a TV or computer. Read books that will engage their imaginations and draw them into the story. Lamplighter Publishing is an excellent resource for such books.
- Challenge your grandkids to a reading contest. Prepare a reading list that you have already approved and ask them to choose books or articles from that list to read over the next month. Offer a special prize (a day at the zoo or a theme park, or a dinner and movie night out) for reading a predetermined number of pages in that month. Make the challenge multiple times a year if you can. If you are long distant, you can tally points that can be used however you decide to use them. Be creative—you have it in you to make it happen.
- Plan a game night with your grandkids if they are nearby or when they come to visit. Set up several game options that everyone can play and have them rotate from one game to the next. When the timer goes off, everyone moves and resumes playing wherever the previous players left off.
- Propose a 24-hour tech-fast challenge. No TV, cell phones, emails, computer games, etc. for a whole day (or whatever time you

choose). Plan several fun and meaningful activities for them to do in place of their devices—puzzles, crafts, scavenger hunt, etc. Ask everyone to write down how they felt about the day. Did they learn anything they might not have learned if they had been connected to their technology toys? What was the hardest part? You'll launch some great discussions.

TRAP #2: Virtual Unreality

My cousin told me about a grandfather he knew who spent an evening out with his grandson. They had dinner and attended a movie together. Throughout the evening, his grandson rarely stopped texting on his cell phone, even during the movie. Irritated, the grandfather thought about snatching the cell phone from him, and giving a good lecture about basic politeness, but he restrained himself. As his grandson was about to exit the car at the end of the evening, grandpa decided to speak.

"I'm going to ask you a question, and I want you to think about it. Don't answer now. We'll talk about it later." He paused, then continued. "Do you think you were with me tonight? Let me know your answer after you've had time to think about it."

The grandfather said good-night and left him to ponder his question. The grandson truly respected his grandfather. He knew him to be a man of honor and integrity, so he took his grandfather's question seriously. The question soon led to a conversation with the rest of his family, who were just as guilty of habitual texting.

The next week the grandson apologized to his grandfather acknowledging his rudeness while they were together. He pledged to be responsible for appropriate uses of his cell phone. They talked freely about the importance of relationships, what it means to be with someone, and how to manage modern technologies like cell phones so that they don't interfere with those relationships. They talked a great deal about what it meant to honor and value others.

Virtual reality, the engaging of a person's mind with an imaginary reality, is not new to the human experience. Theater and the arts employ similar experiences. However, modern technology has unsealed a vast new world of virtual reality beyond just the smartphone or tablet that allows a human to enter an artificially simulated environment generated by computers.

Today's world of digital simulation has propelled us into the unfortunate realm of virtual relationships. Lamplight Publishing founder Mark Hamby calls this phenomenon *virtual unreality*, a much more accurate description, I think. Virtual unreality substitutes face-to-face personal relationships with online virtual connections.

We are witnessing the evolution of a generation lacking the ability to express simple social skills and courtesies. Rising incivility is attributed largely to obsessive, undisciplined uses of technology in social settings where you don't have to look someone in the eye.

Let's face it, social networking sites like Twitter and Facebook don't actually offer a safe place to feel compassion or even admiration. While it is not uncommon for people to have hundreds and even thousands of 'friends' on Facebook, these are mostly mile-wide and inch-deep friendships—vastly removed from the depth of true friendships. Rapper Prince EA has correctly suggested these social networks should be more accurately labeled "anti-social networks."[4]

It's easy to forget that virtual reality is an illusion. The illusion of virtual friendships is that we stay in contact with so many 'friends' online we end up ignoring the real friends and relationships that are in the same room with us. We spend more time talking on the cell phone or chatting online than close face-to-face conversations.

In a 2010 *USA Today* article, Mark Vernon describes close friends as those who "sit with one another across the course of their lives, sharing its savor—its moments, bitter and sweet."[5] He's right. That's because true friendships take time and effort.

Real hands-on relationships are intentional. They sit across from each other and share life. In an age of cyber-relationships, the trap is buying into the lie that a large number of virtual friendships with sound-bite conversations and log-in/log-off connections are a suitable substitute for authentic friendships with real-time connections. In the world of relationships, sometimes less really is more.

TRAP #3: Boredom Syndrome

One of the most common responses I hear from young people today when their technology toys have been taken away or restricted is, "I'm bored." When a kid says that, he is saying he can't find creative and inventive things to do on his own. Kids who are easily bored are addicted to a variety of stimuli needed to hold their interest and keep functioning. Without the extra stimuli, the remaining alternative is to be alone with one's thoughts. That is a terrifying prospect for a lot of kids. Boredom is another deceptive trap of technology.

Boredom sprouts from the loss of contentment and quietude—the ability to be still and at peace. Wonder and imagination have been robbed. A generation is growing up on our watch requiring continuous amusement and external stimuli of some kind. Today's technology generates an unending source of 'noise' drowning out all other voices or thoughts. We are raising a generation uncomfortable with silence and solitude. The ability to meditate and see the wonder in life is sucked out of them by *virtual substitutes*. Smartphones and iPads become alternative solutions to boredom for kids, and adults.

Contemporary education unwittingly contributes to the tech obsession. How? Education relying upon digital resources to 'enhance' children's education leaves our kids largely unexposed to natural imaginative activity.

The Parents Television Council (PTC) warns against too much media that can lead to a host of problems later in life, including intellectual development. "Even programming that is built as educational really has very little educational benefit for the youngster," according to Melissa Henson with PTC. "The child is more likely to grow intellectually and developmentally at a faster pace if they're not watching television and instead are looking at books, playing outside, or engaging with other kids or adults."[6] One high school student describes how he doesn't like to read books or novels because it takes too long. "You can get the whole story in six minutes online," he boasted. "I prefer the immediate gratification."

A constant barrage of stimuli from media technology makes a child's brain more "easily habituated" according to a Kaiser study,[7] and less able to sustain attention. Over time this means it will be more difficult for this generation to stay focused, to complete tasks, or to defer gratification. Easily distracted, kids engrossed in various media are vulnerable to dangerous ideas and thoughtless decisions. This also means that young people obsessed with media technology are more likely to have trouble engaging with matters of faith, truth, and spiritual disciplines.

The spiritual disciplines of prayer, meditation, fasting, and study foster the development of our mind and our ability to relate to others. This is how our Creator intended for our brains to develop. Excessive preoccupation with digital media damages one's ability to center on what is true and excellent. It also makes it difficult to engage in spiritual disciplines which cultivate character and relationship with the Creator.

Clearly, Satan is skilled at manipulating hearts and minds through media technology. Technology is a dangerous trap when discernment and self-control is lacking. When a child is robbed of imagination and wonder, a corruption of the brain occurs that does not know what to do without technological stimulants.

Is it possible to control technology so it does not strip the true delights and wonders of life from us and our children? I think it is. The key is finding creative ways to engage your grandchildren in fun, stimulating activities that will replace the need to be constantly connected digitally. I gave you a few helpful suggestions in the previous chapter.

There's one more trap I believe we dare not cannot ignore.

TRAP #4: Predator Vulnerability

The information currently available on internet predators is frightening. For example, Youth for Christ's *Enough Is Enough* internet safety program information claims that seventy-seven percent of all predator contacts are with teens ages fourteen and older, mostly girls. Twelve percent of teenage girls admitted to eventually meeting strangers in person whom they first met while online. A majority (58 percent) of teens don't see anything wrong with posting personal information and photos of themselves on social networking sites.[8] The most alarming part is that most teens knowingly chat with adult strangers online with little concern. Statistics like these are shocking, to say the least.

Technology does not police itself. It cannot prevent fraud, scams, or emotional terrorism on its own. Predators know how to use the internet and other technologies to prey on the numerous lonely and wounded hearts in our world. Emotional terrorism is the trademark of such predators. They know how desperately people want to feel loved and accepted. Children and teens, especially teenage girls, lacking an environment of love and blessing are particularly vulnerable.

Regardless of the controls you or your grandchildren's parents set up to protect them, if their lives are not being cultivated under the arbor of blessing, the Gospel, and a loving home, they will be exceptionally vulnerable. No level of controls can prevent them from seeking love and acceptance elsewhere if they are not receiving it at home.

Older adults are targets as well. Many older adults avoid any use of the internet because they fear identity theft or becoming unsuspecting victims of deceptive emails and advertising. Older adults often find it difficult to grasp how someone could so cold-heartedly prey on trusting people without any conscience. We forget how wicked the heart of man really is.

Technology has made it possible for people to develop images and brand labels that create the illusion of being something they are not. Wicked men now have a palette of new tools for scamming innocent victims or hacking their personal information. The double-edged sword of technology offers both timesaving advantages as well as the potential for devastating personal losses for you and your grandchildren. Vigilance cannot be minimized or short-changed.

Vigilance is about due diligence for the protection of our grandchildren… and ourselves.

GRANDPAUSE…

THINKING IT THROUGH:

1. Review the four different 'traps' mentioned in this chapter. What information is new for you or something you had not given much thought to prior to reading this section? How has this information changed your view of the dangers technology can present?

2. Of these four 'traps' discussed, which present the greatest challenge for you or your grandchildren? Why?

3. Which of the ideas or suggestions given seem most helpful to you? Which would be unlikely for you to use? Why?

ACTION STEP:

Review the action ideas presented in this chapter. Pick one or two ideas and develop a plan for how you intend to use them with your grandchildren and family. Ask someone you trust to pray with you as you do this then let that person know how it was received.

PART FIVE

STEP UP!

"When I saw their fear, I rose and spoke to the nobles, the officials and the rest of the people: 'Do not be afraid of them; remember the Lord who is great and awesome, and fight for your brothers, your sons, your daughters, your wives and your houses.'" (Nehemiah 4:14, NASB)

***

A delegation from the tribe of Judah, led by Caleb son of Jephunneh the Kenizzite, came to Joshua at Gilgal. Caleb said to Joshua, "Remember what the LORD said to Moses, the man of God, about you and me when we were at Kadesh-barnea. I was forty years old when Moses, the servant of the LORD, sent me from Kadesh-barnea to explore the land of Canaan. I returned and gave from my heart a good report, but my brothers who went with me frightened the people and discouraged them from entering the Promised Land. For my part, I followed the LORD my God completely. So that day Moses promised me, 'The land of Canaan on which you were just walking will be your special possession and that of your descendants forever, because you wholeheartedly followed the LORD my God.'

"Now, as you can see, the LORD has kept me alive and well as he promised for all these forty-five years since Moses made this promise—even while Israel wandered in the wilderness. Today I am eighty-five years old. I am as strong now as I was when Moses sent me on that journey, and I can still travel and fight as well as I could then. So I'm asking you to give me the hill country that the LORD promised

me. You will remember that as scouts we found the Anakites living there in great, walled cities. But if the LORD is with me, I will drive them out of the land, just as the LORD said."

So Joshua blessed Caleb son of Jephunneh and gave Hebron to him as an inheritance. Hebron still belongs to the descendants of Caleb son of Jephunneh, the Kenizzite, because he wholeheartedly followed the LORD, the God of Israel. (Joshua 14:6-14, NLT)

16

Are You a Repristinator or Reposer?

"We are the salt of the earth, not the sugar, and our ministry is truly to cleanse and not just to change the taste."
–Vance Havner

My grandparents used to have a white picket fence across the front yard of their house. I loved that fence. I remember a few years after Grandpa had passed away that white picket fence began to look a little worse for wear. The paint was peeling and some pickets had cracked or were broken. That's what happens when something is left to the natural process of deterioration.

Then one day my father came to the house with a hammer and a bucket of white paint. Before long that picket fence looked like it was supposed to look—a bright, cheery adornment for Grandma's front yard. It had been *repristinated*—restored to its original condition!

Repristinate may not be familiar to you, but it is a real word. According to Webster's, to *repristinate* is "to restore something to its original state or condition." I wonder if it would be accurate to say that one of the responsibilities God has given grandparents is that of a *repristinator* (that's my word). God has given us the experiences and tools required to restore the worse-for-wear culture we helped create back to its original condition according to God's design. On the other hand, we could choose to be *reposers* (my word again), who lie around like we're dead and do nothing.

Our worldview determines what we perceive as valid and valued. It will ultimately move us to be either *reprisinators* or *reposers*. History suggests that if at least 10 percent of any culture hold an unshakable belief in something, the majority of that society will also embrace that belief. The kind of unshakable belief that influences a society or culture with such power involves more than personal opinions.

Unshakable belief is a deep conviction formed out of a worldview that moves us toward a visible way of doing life. It is so vibrant that it catches the attention of the culture in which we live. It's the process of *repristination…* and knowing what to do.

As followers of Christ we hold a conviction about who God is and the world He made. We believe He created us for Himself, and that He paid the ultimate price to restore us to a personal relationship with Him. He made a way for us to avoid the judgment that would otherwise be inescapable. It's called the Gospel, and it changes everything. The Gospel transforms hearts and minds under a new covenant of grace and atonement.

Our unshakable faith in God's truth is the basis for a wisdom to understand the times. It compels us to act with compassion in the power of the Holy Spirit to draw others to Christ and His salvation. Our deepest desire is to make much of Him, His goodness and His truth.

According to Genesis 1:27-28, we are called to live as redemptive agents who, made in the image of God, rule, produce, reproduce, and steward the earth. We were reborn to that purpose through the Gospel. The Gospel cannot be reduced to a free pass to heaven with a license to live like the rest of the world.

Chuck Colson suggested that Christ's disciples are commissioned, not only to make disciples, but to serve as God's agents in "sustaining and renewing creation, defending the created institutions of family and society, and exposing false worldviews."[1] In other words, the new birth is only the starting point for true disciples, albeit the critical and essential starting point. Indeed, it is the miracle of a new life that compels Christ's disciples to engage the world with the whole truth and make disciples who do the same.

Jesus came to testify to the truth. We are to do the same. While defending, proclaiming, and authenticating the Truth exposes the Lie, I am convinced that no amount of carefully crafted persuasion or reason, though valuable, will engage the world and cause it to change. It is the incarnation of truth by people of unshakable faith that will open the door for the Holy Spirit to convict the world.

Such unshakable faith is displayed where we live and work in the marketplace, the laboratory, the classroom, the neighborhood, and the home. If we are to be effective agents of change, our lives must display the glory of what ought to be. Only then will the Holy Spirit work through us to transform and re-make our culture. Nice theology, but what does it mean?

Fight for Our Families

Unshakable faith is proactive. Remember Nehemiah. Amid opposition and fear, he called the faithful to not be afraid, but to *"Remember the Lord, who is great and glorious, and fight for your friends, your families, and your homes!"* (Nehemiah 4:14)

Confident in God's ability to do the impossible, he stood before a fearful people and gave them a reason to hope. They did not need to fear, he told them, because "our God will fight for us" (Neh. 4:20). Nehemiah understood what was going on. He knew God was in charge, and what God wanted him to do. Then, he did it.

We also must fight for our families, which means we must not only understand the times, but know what to do, and do it. Much of our struggle with knowing what to do arises from emotions and feelings that sabotage our confidence to discern what is right. We feel incompetent to choose the right course of action. It is especially hard when so many voices tell us to *follow our heart* and do what *feels* right.

The problem with following your heart is that the heart is subjective and easily manipulated. Following your heart is not the best test for determining what is right (Jeremiah 17:9). Feelings focus on circumstances more than the truth. Emotions and feelings easily distract from what is obvious. Knowing what to do in times like this requires wisdom, not feelings.

Clearly, feelings are part of being human, but when feelings displace discernment, poor decisions almost always follow. Merchandisers understand this, and they have learned to use it effectively to convince us to purchase things we would not normally buy. They know that our feelings will often overrule sound judgment.

Wisdom is not driven by feelings, but by truth. The source of all wisdom is God, and we find it through knowledge of His Word that is put into practice. *"Your word is a lamp to my feet and a light for my path"* (Psalm 119:109).

The problem may not be a matter of knowing what to do, but not believing what God says is really what He means. Or we may wonder whether the Bible is relevant to life in the 21st century. On perhaps you simply do not know what the Bible says.

Knowing what to do is not a philosophical exercise, or a matter for professionals to decide for us. How is it the men of Issachar possessed the wisdom to know what to do? The Bible doesn't tell us, but I suspect these men knew the writings of Moses and were astute in how they applied what they knew to what was going on around them. I suspect they were wise in good ole common sense as well.

Six Practical "To-Do's"

While there are no A+B+C formulas for knowing what to do, I know at least six effective things any believer can do in times like this. The first three are clear biblical commands. The final three are simply common sense.

1. **Study the Word**
   "Do you best [study] to present yourself to God as one approved, a workman who does not need to be ashamed and who correctly handles the word of truth" (2 Timothy 2:15).

"All Scripture is God-breathed and is useful for teaching, rebuking, correcting and training in righteousness, so that the man [or woman] of God may be thoroughly equipped for every good work" (2 Timothy 3:16-17).

"Do not conform any longer to the pattern of this world, but be transformed by the renewing of your mind [studying, learning what is true]. Then you will be able to test and approve what God's will is—His good, pleasing and perfect will" (Romans 12:2).

"Your Word is a lamp to my feet and a light for my path" (Psalms 119:105).

2. **Pray fervently for wisdom**

"If any of you lacks wisdom, he should ask God, who gives generously to all without finding fault, and it will be given to him. But when he asks, he must believe and not doubt…" (James 1:5-6).

"I keep asking that the God of our Lord Jesus Christ, the glorious Father, may give you the spirit of wisdom and revelation, so that you may know Him better. I pray also that the eyes of your heart may be enlightened in order that you may know the hope to which He has called you, the riches of His glorious inheritance in the saints, and His incomparably great power for us who believe" (Ephesians 1:17-19).

"We have not stopped praying for you and asking God to fill you with the knowledge of His will through all spiritual wisdom and understanding. And we pray this in order that you may live a life worthy of the Lord and may please Him in every way: bearing fruit in every good work, growing in the knowledge of God, being strengthened with all power according to His glorious might so that you may have great endurance and patience, and joyfully giving thanks to God the Father…" (Colossians 1:9-12).

3. **Fellowship regularly with other believers**
    "Let us not give up meeting together, as some are in the habit of doing, but let us encourage one another—and all the more as you see the Day approaching" (Hebrews 10:25).

    "It was He who gave some to be apostles, some to be prophets, some to be evangelists, and some to be pastors and teachers to prepare God's people for works of service, so that the body of Christ may be built up until we all reach unity in the faith and in the knowledge of the Son of God, and become mature, attaining to the whole measure of the fullness of Christ. Then we will no long be infants, tossed back and forth by the waves, and blown here and there by every wind of teaching and by the cunning and craftiness of men in their deceitful scheming. Instead, speaking the truth in love, we will in all things grow up into Him who is the Head, that is Christ. From Him the whole body, joined and held together by every supporting ligament, grows and builds itself up in love, as each part does its work" (Ephesians 4:11-6).

    I cannot say it any plainer that what God has already said. Those who follow Christ are those who put His truths into practice. If we want wisdom, we need to be students of the Word, fervent prayer warriors, and faithful members of a community of believers.

    Now, for a few common-sense suggestions, each focused on getting to the truth when the truth is under fire.

4. **Listen well and learn to ask good questions**
    A lot of false ideas and beliefs are propagated through terminology that is not clearly defined or mis-defined. Learn to listen well so you hear what others are saying. Listening also promotes trust and a sense that you are a safe place to be transparent.

    Learn to pay attention to words like love, marriage, tolerance and truth that may be redefined or undefined in conversations with others. Many people of all ages buy into statements and terms without asking the kind of questions that dig down to whether they are true or not.

Here are six questions that work in many situations where it is important to probe sources and evidences to see if they hold water:

- That's interesting. What do you mean by that? (define terms)
- Where did you get that information? (Are the sources reliable?)
- How do you know it's true? (supporting evidence/facts)
- What if you're wrong? (What are the consequences?)
- What if you're right? (What are the consequences?)
- Would you be willing to explore this further together? (This is important)

Your teen and young adult grandchildren are often so inundated with cultural messages and ideas that little attention is given to whether what they hear or see is actually true. Create a safe place for them to ask the hard questions without feeling judged. Being quick to listen and slow to speak (James 1:19). And when you do speak, speak not to tell, but to test—helping them test to see what is really true.

The third part of James' injunction—slow to anger—will go a long way to creating a safe environment.

5. **Read good books, listen to sound teaching/music**

Not only is this a good idea for you, it is also a good activity to do with your grandchildren. Fill yourself up with what is true, noble, right, pure, lovely, admirable, excellent and praiseworthy (See Philippians 4:8).

If you want to know what to do, learn from others and pursue what is true and praiseworthy. There are so many excellent resources out there rooted in Scripture to help you. You have heard it many times: you will recognize a counterfeit more readily when you have studied the real thing carefully. You can't learn what to do when you're only exposed to things that you should not be doing in the first place.

6. Check your heart

Jesus said, "Where your treasure is, there your heart will be also" (Matthew 6:21). That's why the Bible warns us to "above all else, guard your heart for it is the wellspring of life" (Proverbs 4:23). What are the real treasures that shape your heart--things that matter for eternity, or things that rust and decay? When the bumper sticker on the back of your RV says, "I'm spending my kids' inheritance", I think they will figure out where your true treasures lie.

Inter-Generational Table Talk

The family Thanksgiving dinner was finished, and the plates cleared. The adults sat at the table sharing opinions about current events and issues of the day. Fourteen-year-old Chad remained at the table listening with interest as the adults talked. After listening intently for a while, Chad offered a comment on the subject being discussed. His mother interrupted. "Just go play with the rest of the kids, Chad. This is an adult conversation."

There are few more potent places where intergenerational relationships are cultivated, and significant learning happens, than at the family table. We lose those moments when, like Chad's mother, we forget that.

One of my favorite TV programs is *Blue Bloods*. I enjoy the police drama and relational elements of the show. But what I love most is the scene in every episode when four generations of Reagans sit around the dinner table and talk about life. Great-Grandpa, Grandpa, parents, children—each is included in the conversation. Everyone's input and questions are valued. It's a moving picture of intentional inter-generational learning. It is also a reminder of what's missing in too many families today. Let's bring the family table back to where it belongs for the sake of our children.

I know it's hard when families are constantly going in different directions. The lure of worldly pursuits pulls families in every direction except together. Grandparents, you can set a better example for bringing the generations together at the family table.

I believe God established and ordained a *truth narrative* from which each generation lives, learns, and gives to one another as a family. Psalm 78 describes the expectation God has for parents and grandparents to tell the next generations the Big Story. It is a story that matters to all of us. This biblical notion of family supported by the body of Christ is at the heart of this Gospel shaped narrative in which all things are made new.

Grandparents, we have an opportunity to impact culture. It begins in our own families. Restore the family table and avoid the 'two-table' mentality when your family gathers for important events at Thanksgiving, Christmas, or any other family gathering. You know what I'm talking about—the adult table in one place, the kids' table in another. Protect the family table and seize the opportunities to engage every generation in conversations about life—not segregate them.

Now is the time for courageous grandparents everywhere to step to the plate (or to the table) and intentionally live out this foundational truth designed to bless us all: *From him [Christ] the <u>whole body</u>, joined and held together by every supporting ligament, grows and builds itself up in love, <u>as each part does its work</u>* (Ephesians 4:16).

Each part cannot do its work if we are not together!

GRANDPAUSE...

THINKING IT THROUGH:

1. What is the difference between a *repristinator* and a *'reposer'*? Which would your grandchildren or adult children say you are? Which would *you* say that you are?

2. Which of the six practical way suggested in this chapter do you find most difficult to practice? Why? Which do you find the easiest? Why?

3. Read through Nehemiah 4. What was the nature of the opposition that Nehemiah and the people of Jerusalem faced in their task of building the wall? What is the nature of opposition we face today? What does it look like to "fight" for your family in today's world?

ACTION STEPS:

1. An example of how four young men lived in the culture thrust upon them.

2. Read Nehemiah 4:14. Decide what you will do to implement at least one of the ideas generated by question #3. Ask someone to pray with you that God will give you wisdom and courageous resolve to implement them according to His grace and for His glory.

17

Take Back the Hill Country

"Nothing can cure us of fear till God cures us of unbelief."
–Francis Burkitt

Caleb, son of Jephunneh, is one of my heroes. He was the kind of man I want to be. He had a passion for living and a wholehearted commitment to believing and serving God no matter how dangerous that might be. You know his story. It happened long before Nehemiah—before the walls of Jerusalem, the Temple, and the kings of Israel.

Selected by Moses as one of twelve elite reconnaissance team members assigned to spy out the land, Caleb took his assignment seriously. After completing their exploration of the land, the twelve returned to report their findings.

About this much they were all in agreement—the land was indeed filled with abundant goodness just as God said. The amazing samples of the bountiful fruit they brought back confirmed God's promise of a land flowing with milk and honey.

Concerning the rest of God's promise, however, the team was not united. Overshadowing God's assurance that the inhabitants could be defeated were unmistakable realities staring them in the face. Not only were there a lot people, but they were huge, giant-sized people. Only Caleb and Joshua believed God and stood in opposition to the popular opinion expressed by the other ten. Ten of the twelve wanted to play it safe; two believed God would defeat their enemy. The trepidation of the ten spread like a plague throughout the camp of Israel, causing the people to cave in to the fear expressed by the ten.

Whoa, hold on there! Are we missing something here? Aren't these the same people who had recently witnessed incredible miracles of God since leaving Egypt? Hadn't they seen God part the sea so they could cross on dry ground? Weren't they the ones who stood safely on the other side of that same sea and watched God unleash the parted waters to drown Pharaoh's pursuing army? Surely, they had not forgotten the daily reminders of God's presence in the pillar of fire by night and a cloud by day. Hadn't they experienced God's goodness as He quenched their parched throats with water from the rock and satisfied their hunger with manna and quail? How can someone witness such amazing things firsthand and get hung up on a few oversized Anakites?

At any rate, the scouts made their report: *"The land we explored devours those living in it. All the people we saw there are of great size… we seemed like grasshoppers in our own eyes and we looked the same to them"* (Num. 13:32-33). Their ability to evaluate their circumstances in terms of who they were and who their God was had been blurred by fear driving them to unbelief. It was too radical a leap for them to believe God could do something this big even though He had already proven Himself quite capable in big things. How short our memories can be.

From our vantage point it's difficult to understand how, after all God had done getting them to this point, they couldn't trust Him to finish the job. After all, God appeared to Moses in the burning bush and gave him these promises: 1) He would rescue them from the hand of the Egyptians; and 2) He would bring them into a "good and spacious land, a land flowing with milk and honey." The "good and spacious land" now lay before them just as God had promised. Now they stood paralyzed, unwilling to take action to claim that promise.

Before we point fingers and shake our heads at these foolish Israelites, we might want to look in the mirror. I suspect there are a few giants in our lives that strike terror in our hearts and keep us from following God's call. Fear has a way of evaporating our confidence in God's promises. Sometimes it's easier to quietly yield to popular opinion than to speak up and do what is right.

If it's true, as research suggests, that only 10 percent of a society holding an unshakable belief can lead that society to adopt its belief, then why has the Christian community been so impotent to impact our society? According to the Chuck Colson Center for Christian Worldview, less than 10 percent of Americans make up the cultural elite of our society. Yet they are the ones we hear about, read about, and see in the media dictating what is politically correct.

Grandparents, who claim to be Christians in this nation, amount to close to ten percent of our population. Why are *we* not the cultural influencers in our society? Is it possible for us to override the influence of the postmodern cultural elitists? That depends.

If our faith in the God of Heaven is unshakable in every area of life, then there is no doubt God can still turn the world upside down. If we lived with a resolve not to be intimidated into silence, but to unite and stand up for what is right and true, imagine the light that would shine in the darkness. So much depends upon how courageously we proclaim and live out the Gospel by the power of the Spirit with authenticity, compassion, and grace—seasoned, of course, with salt.

Ending the Spiral of Silence

We live in a time when the majority often cowers in silence as those few who wield the power to shape public thought and policy bully their way through society using intimidation to achieve their goals. I mentioned Neumann's "spiral of silence" theory in Chapter 13. Her theory asserts that people are less likely to voice their opinion on a topic if they sense they are in the minority, especially if they fear reprisal from the majority.

In other words, when those in control spin their views on social issues to shape public opinion on that issue, the majority, even if they disagree, will sit in silence once they perceive the matter has been decided. Most people will concede the issue because of the fear rejection or isolation from the mainstream.

A 2009 study entitled, *The False Enforcement of Unpopular Norms,* at the University of California, Berkley, describes false enforcement as the pressure to conform to a norm not otherwise accepted.[1] This is illustrated by the familiar Hans Christian Andersen fable, *The Emperor's New Clothes.*

In this well-known tale of a naked emperor, his tailors convince him that his new suit of clothes will be invisible to anyone in his realm who is stupid, incompetent, or unfit for his court. Not wanting to be labeled as such, his court goes along with the ruse and manipulates the masses to do the same, even though everyone knows the truth. No one wants to risk speaking the truth for fear of reprisal by the emperor. That has a familiar ring to it.

Following the courageous example of the small child who finally spoke up and declared, "But he isn't wearing anything at all," it's time for this generation to speak up and tell the truth. We must wake up, wise up, and step up to counter the delusion under which we have lived for too long. It may take a few courageous grandparents to lead the charge and tell the emperor he is naked.

God has already declared that we have everything we need by His divine power for life and godliness (see 2 Peter 1:3). We do not have to be enslaved to the spiral of silence. We are free by the power of God to launch a movement that will speak out for the sake of our grandchildren and the glory of God.

Is speaking the truth risky and dangerous? Absolutely! Seemingly insurmountable obstacles and risks are part of life, especially when we are pursuing God's agenda. Wholehearted followers of Christ know there are dangers. Fear is still our greatest enemy.

Fear is constantly poised to warp our perspective of reality, numb our hearts, and intimidate us into silence. Fear dupes us into believing we can embrace a "safe faith"—whatever that means. Living out a genuine, unshakable faith is never safe, but it is right. God is faithful, trustworthy, and bigger than any danger we might encounter, and that is the reason we can take the risk.

It's time to shed the lie that we can play it safe and win. We need not fear those defining moments God sets before us. Our vision should not be fixated on the dangers and risks involved. Rather, we *"fix on our eyes on Jesus, the author and perfecter of our faith, who for the joy set before him endured the cross"* (Hebrews 12:2). This is the reason we do not grow weary or lose heart. Before us are amazing opportunities for God to display His glory and might. If fear wins, the next generations lose. Are you willing to allow that to happen on your watch? I'm not.

Worry, fear, anxiety—these are the things that shift our eyes from God to our circumstances. It was what Caleb had to battle with his cohorts. Nehemiah had to deal with it too as Sanballat and his co-conspirators attempted to intimidate the Jews trying to rebuild the wall. Nehemiah refused to be intimidated because he knew the Lord was fighting for him and the people. He reminded them of God's promise and why they were doing what they were doing. This was a struggle for their families and homes. It will be no less so for you and me today.

Fear of Failing

Perhaps you struggle with doubt seeping its way into your thoughts. You may find yourself asking, *What if I fail?* So what if you do? Someone once wisely said, "Failure is the context for miracles." If you never step out in faith and take a risk, you may delude yourself into thinking the safest route is the best choice. But it rarely is.

The safe path is, in fact, a dead-end path paved with fear and apathy. If you surrender to intimidation, you embark on a road that diverts you from the opportunity to show your family and the world the greatness of God. You will also allow the enemy to breach the defenses around your family.

That's what I love about Caleb. Caleb understood the risks. He chose to remain resolute in his belief that God is able to do what He promised

He would do. He knew that, in spite of the dangers and obstacles, God had already promised to give them the land. He believed God, not men.

Forty years later Caleb stood before Joshua and asked for the land God had promised to him. His courageous, wholehearted commitment to God compelled him to declare, *"So here I am today, eighty-five years old! I am still as strong today as the day Moses sent me out;* **I'm just as vigorous to go out to battle now as I was then.** *Now give me this hill country that the Lord promised me that day. You yourself heard then that the Anakites were there and their cities were large and fortified, but, the Lord helping me, I will drive them out just as he said"* (Joshua 14:10-11; emphasis mine).

I don't know about you, but when I read this, my response is "Wow"! Here was a man with a resolute, audacious, and deliberate belief that God would do what He promised no matter how big the obstacles seemed. Caleb wasn't interested in wasting his life by playing it safe. He was not afraid of danger. He was ready to do battle, even at eighty-five, because He believed God was bigger than any giant he might face. He also believed there was too much at stake to sit and do nothing.

What battle is worth fighting today? We may not be sent into harm's way to fight terrorists like our brave young men and women in the military are asked to do. But we still have a battle to fight against a different kind of terrorism—a terrorism of truth. And like Caleb and Nehemiah of long ago, we too are fighting for our brothers, sisters, sons, daughters, husbands, wives, and homes. Grandparents, you are needed on the front lines in this battle.

Our mission is to take back the hill country the enemy gained on our watch. It does not matter if you are a long-distance grandparent, a grandparent raising your grandchildren, a new grandparent, or a grandparent with a quiver filled with grandchildren, you are called to active duty for another generation.

This is a cause for truth and righteousness. It is a cause for the hearts and minds of our grandchildren. This is the point where the courageous do what is right. They sign up for the job of fighting for our homes and our country.

We cannot afford to play it safe and settle back into a comfortable retirement. To play it safe is to assume the greatest risk of all—a wasted life that leaves nothing of value to the next generations. John Piper put it this way: "If our single, all-embracing passion is to make much of Christ in life and death, and if the life that magnifies Him most is the life of costly love, then life is risk, and risk is right. To run from it is to waste your life."[2]

These are turbulent and uncertain times requiring radical solutions by a courageous people with an unshakable faith in Jesus Christ. This battle does not require intimidation and fear as our weapons of influence. Dr. Haddon Robinson, Distinguished Professor at Gordon-Conwell Theological Seminary, rightly said, "If we are committed to a 'cause' but remain unconcerned with Christ, we may trade away the power of God for the power of politics."[3]

In Christ, we have weapons unlike any other. *"The weapons we fight with are not weapons of the world. On the contrary, they have divine power to demolish strongholds. We demolish arguments and every pretension that sets itself up against the knowledge of God, and we take captive every thought to make it obedient to Christ"* (2 Cor. 10:4-5).

Our Deployment Orders

Grandparents, your deployment orders have been issued. Will you sign up and step up as Christ's ambassadors and soldiers for the sake of the next generations? There is so much at stake if you don't.

Here are five components of our deployment orders that will help us make fulfill God's mission for us. This is where the rubber meets the road. No more talk—let's go to work. What are we to do? Here are our orders:

1. **PRAY**…pray, pray in your own closet. Pray with other believers as often as you can. If you aren't already part of a group of grandparents who are praying regularly for the next generations and our families, organize a G@)P (Grandparents At Prayer) group your area to encourage grandparents to join together in prayer. Jesus said, *"Where*

two or three are come together in my name, there I am with them" (Matthew 18:20).

Corporate prayer is powerful. When two or more unite their hearts with the Father's, the floodgates of Heaven are opened. Very little corporate praying happens in American churches today. Determined grandparents can change that, so let's do it. Get a copy of Lillian Penner's book, *Grandparenting with a Purpose: Effective Ways to Pray for Your Grandchildren*[4] if you need some good ideas. Revival is the fruit of fervent praying. Visit our website for more information.

2. **REPENT!** Praying is not merely petition. It is also a time to allow God to search our hearts and expose any wicked ways or motives. Repentance means owning up to our sins, both individually and as a people. Courageous grandparents accept that responsibility because we know that personal and corporate revival originate in repentance. Repentance acknowledges that we have strayed from the truth and the paths of righteousness, and we have not taught our children as we ought. It starts with us—dealing with the sin and rebellion in our own lives. True repentance changes course of our lives and becomes the pipeline through which God's transforming power of grace and truth is unleashed in our culture.

   Once more Nehemiah sets an example for us to follow. Upon learning of the condition of his homeland, he wept and went to his knees to confess the sins of Israel. He did this before he asked God's favor to win over the king.

   In the same way we must acknowledge our guilt. At times we have compromised when we should have stood our ground. We have remained silent when we should have spoken out. We have embraced a life of selfishness and greed when we should have looked to the interests of others, especially the poor. Too often, we are guilty of "dumbing down" the Gospel and allowing evil to weasel its way into our homes.

When we humble ourselves and repent, God makes a promise: *"If my people will pray, and humble themselves, and turn from their wicked ways, then will I hear from heaven," says the Lord God* (2 Chronicles 7:14). We would be foolish to allow pride to stand in the way of God's promise to pour out His blessing.

3. **SPEAK OUT**: God will work through even a lone voice. That's what He did through men like Wilberforce and Wesley, Nehemiah and Caleb. How much more might God move in people's hearts when the voices of thousands upon thousands speak out to proclaim the truth. How do you do that?

    - One way we can speak out is to organize a *Courageous Grandparenting* group in your community. Gather like-minded grandparents and parents to study God's Word, to pray, and to stimulate one another to be God's culture-makers for a time such as this.
    - Talk to your pastor(s) about the importance of grandparenting in family discipleship. Ask about bringing a Courageous Grandparenting Seminar or Gospel Shaped Family conference to your church or community. Visit our website listed in the back of this book for more information.

4. **CONNECT INTER-GENERATIONALLY**: Courageous grandparents seek opportunities to engage with their grandchildren and other children, youth and young adults in their sphere of influence. Consider these possibilities:

    - Get involved in the children's ministry in your church. I recently asked a group of senior adults to get involved in the children's ministry in their church once a month.

      As you may have guessed, I got no takers to my invitation. I did get some responses along the lines of: "I already did my time"; "I'm too old to work with kids. Leave that to the younger folks." Sound familiar?

At what age are we too old to contribute to a child's life? And who came up with the notion that raising kids or working with children is about 'doing time'? Ministry to kids isn't a prison sentence—it's an opportunity to live joyfully for something more important than our own convenience. It's a chance to be a conduit of God's grace for the next generations.

I'm involved with the AWANA program in my home church. It is one of the most rewarding things I do. Sure, it is challenging at times, but I love working with the grade school-aged children I see each week. I love teaching them God's Word and talking to them about the Gospel. It doesn't get any better than that!

- Take your grandchildren to GrandCamp (www.grandcamps. org) or create your own version of GrandCamp or Cousins Camp. We've even created a *Do-It-Yourself Field Guide* to help you. Jim and Gwen, who helped write the Field Guide say, "The Christian faith of our grandchildren is much deeper largely due to the experiences with us at GrandCamp. For example, after spending just two days at GrandCamp, one granddaughter exclaimed, 'Grandma, GrandCamp is so much fun, and it's so much FUN learning about GOD!'"

- Never settle for being merely a *good* grandparent! Choose to be a courageous, biblical grandparent. Be intentional and diligent about your family's well-being and eternal destiny. Invest in your grandchildren and spend time with them. Explore, debate, create, and serve together. If you are long-distant, find a way to stay in touch regularly.

- Challenge the leadership of your church to promote more

inter-generational dialogue and discussion events. For example, propose a weekend inter-generational retreat where you can sit down and discuss some social issues of our day and what God has to say about them. Or consider doing a Grand Day Out event at your church for grandparents and their grandchildren. Visit www.grandcamps.org to find out more about Grand Day Out events.

- *Do The Right Thing*: The Colson Center for Christian Worldview and the Witherspoon Institute have co-produced a DVD curriculum suitable for use with a small groups, a class, or even a family reunion. The series explores and examines matters of ethics and character relating to home, school, and the workplace. It is a wonderful tool for inter-generational dialogue. Visit www.doingtherightthing.com for more information.

5. **ASK GOOD QUESTIONS**: On matters of faith and morality do not be surprised when people are not receptive to civilized dialogue. In such situations, it is important to be a sincere listener and gracious communicator. James says that we are to be *"quick to listen, slow to speak and slow to become angry"* (James 1:19).

When dealing with hot topic issues like abortion, sexual identity, same-sex marriage, and so forth, earn the right to be heard by being a gracious listener and using kind words. Asking good questions helps build trust and meaningful dialogue, but you become a listener, not a preacher.

Your grandchildren need to know that they will not be condemned if they take a position on an issue you know is wrong. Let truth be seasoned with grace so the Spirit is free to do the work of conviction. Review the questions that were suggested in Chapter 16.

Affirm their value as human beings made in God's image.

Communicate your love whatever they choose to do. With gentleness and kindness also let them know that on matters in which the Scriptures are clear, you will stand upon the authority of God's Word.

Compassionate Engagement

These five action steps are radical in many ways, but Life with a capital 'L' in which Christ lives in me is anything but cozy. Those who choose to embrace these action steps with courageous faith will position themselves to be Christ's powerful conduits of grace and change.

While you may desire the greatest good for those you love, not all will want what you want. Expect opposition along the way from those who don't get it or don't want to get it. Let your charity remain steadfast always. Dr. Mark Young, President of Denver Seminary, said it this way: "Passionate belief must never eclipse compassionate engagement with those who do not see the truth as we see it."[5] Nor, I might add, for those who do not want to see the truth at all.

Our family has had to face this with a man who is very dear to us. Trevor (not his real name) is a self-proclaimed homosexual. He announced his same-sex 'marriage' to his gay partner on Facebook. When some family and Christian 'friends' did not post congratulations to him on his page, he responded with some intense anger. He announced he was 'unfriending' all the hateful, negative people on his list who did not offer congratulations.

Attempts to respond to him graciously were not well received. In fact, he was clearly hostile. There was no desire on the part of those who did not agree with his chosen lifestyle to abandon the friendship. In fact, they were eager to continue it. Unfortunately, Trevor was not receptive to any position other than his own on the matter.

In fact, conditions were laid out for any acceptable relationship on his part. Those who would affirm and support his same-sex marriage publicly would be welcome. All others would be cut off. No allowance was made for disagreement or a different point of view. It was all or nothing.

For some in our family, this was an experience very much like the death of a dear friend. Even after one final plea to not terminate the friendship, Trevor's demands remained firm. My daughter, who was quite close, responded very graciously and let him know that her friendship and love for him would never be tied to conditions, even if he felt otherwise. She could not, however, abandon her faith and convictions about God's moral law simply to meet his demands. She would remain a friend without conditions, welcoming any opportunity to reconnect. In the end, he had nothing else to say.

Nehemiah was no stranger to hostility and opposition. When faced with intense opposition, Nehemiah responded by going to God in prayer because he knew this was the Lord's battle. Armed with wisdom for the moment, he took the appropriate action to deal with the opposition and continue the work. His charge to the people was to "remember the Lord, who is great and awesome…. Our God will fight for us." With that perspective, they finished the wall in fifty-two days. Those who opposed them had nothing left to say.

We must never rest or desert the fight because of opposition. I will not give up until I have done all that God asks of me to stir this generation of current and emerging Christian grandparents into courageous action. Imagine with me what an army of faithful grandparents could do in the power of the Holy Spirit to champion the Gospel and turn our world upside down. Can you imagine?

I believe my assignment is to remind you and grandparents everywhere of what's at stake if we don't wake up and step up in response to God's call to live for the next generations. I challenge you to take up the cause with me for our grandchildren's sake—for the sake of every child, teen, and young adult being taken captive to the Lie. May God open your eyes to the opportunity of your lifetime.

I have one more chapter left. I've written this specifically to men because I believe the presence of a father/grandfather in a child's life is vital. Grandmothers, you are critical too, but God has designed fathers and grandfathers with a disproportionate impact upon a child—for good or ill.

Grandma, will you encourage your husband and other fathers in your family to at least read this chapter? And God bless you mothers and grandmothers who stay the course and also do battle for your families. You rock!

GRANDPAUSE...

THINKING IT THROUGH:

1. What are some giants you face when it comes to being intentional with your grandchildren in matters of faith and the Gospel? Do you identify more with Caleb or the ten who worried about all the challenges? Why?

2. Of the five suggestions (pray, repent, speak out, connect inter-generationally, ask good questions), which is the hardest for you to do? Which is the easiest? Why?

3. Is there someone in your family that you find it difficult to speak with about certain social issues? Why do you think so many grandparents fear speaking the truth about some of these issues? Why is political correctness so dangerous and destructive? How ought we to respond?

4. Read 2 Timothy 3:1-5; 4:3-4. What does it look like to be "strong and courageous" in such times? Is it possible to change a culture that turns its back on the truth? Why or why not?

ACTION STEPS:

1. Make a list of the things that create fear and discouragement in your life. Lay the list before God and confess your fears. Now ask Him to replace your fear with courage and resolve to do what is right and speak the truth boldly.

2. Taking the hill country also involves linking arms with others who are willing to join the battle. Caleb did not go into battle alone. Using Paul's instruction in 2 Timothy 4:2, develop a strategy for engaging your families and your sphere of influence with the truth about the Gospel.

3. Pray for one another as you step out in faith to be strong and courageous.

18

The Unique Impact of a Grandfather

*"Men are God's method. The Church is looking for better
methods; God is looking for better men."*
–E. M. Bounds

As part of a small Midwestern church Christmas program, the adult leaders asked young Ben questions about his family and interesting things about himself. At one point, someone asked, "Who is your hero?" Without hesitation, he loudly proclaimed, "My dad!"

When I hear a child make that kind of declaration, it warms my heart and brings tears to my eyes. What father wouldn't burst with pride to hear his son make such a declaration. Yet, when I realize the only heroes many kids and teens have are celebrities who promote values and attitudes that ought to alarm any parent or grandparent, it breaks my heart. The main reason these celebrities achieve hero status with young people is because the heroes they truly need and desire are lacking—Dads and Granddads.

I have written this chapter because I want you to know that as a grandfather you matter. In fact, you matter in two ways. You matter as a father to your adult children and their spouses, and you also matter as a grandfather to your grandchildren.

I know this word, *"matter"*, is overused and misused, so let's be clear about what it means. Every human being matters because we are all, male and female, made in the image of God. We matter to God, which is why he became a man to show His love for us. We matter because God created us with value and purpose.

But there's another sense of mattering. For example, men and women matter in the lives of their children and grandchildren in different ways. While both men and women influence a child, the influence of a father or grandfather in a child's life is uniquely impactful. It can never be overstated, but it is commonly under-estimated.

A Kenyan proverb says, "The village that fails to initiate its boys into manhood will see those same boys <u>burn down the village just to feel the heat</u>." If you substitute *fathers* and *grandfathers* for 'village,' I think you have a more accurate statement.

This proverb is correct about one thing. When boys become adults without other men, like a father or grandfather, to teach them who they are and why they are here, instead of becoming men who protect, they become thugs who destroy and hurt others. Violence is one way they can feel the heat. A father or grandfather's impact is also huge in a girl's life, but most girls who become women with a wounded sense of value or identity are more likely to harm themselves than others.

Anyone in prison ministry will tell you that young men who grow up in homes without fathers are twice as likely to end up in jail as those who come from traditional two-parent families. According to Prison Fellowship, more than "seventy percent of juveniles in state-operated institutions come from fatherless homes."[1] More recent research places that percentage between seventy-six and eighty-five percent.

The void of godly **paternal** influences in the home is a serious matter. How does a boy learn about manhood if there is no man in his life to teach him and show him? I agree with my friend, Craig Glass, founder of Peregrine Ministries, when he says that men have a *disproportionate* impact on a child's sense of identity and purpose compared to mothers. "Men matter precisely because the consequences of the character choices they make differ so significantly [from women]. Good men bring blessing to families and society; wicked men bring multiplied destruction."[2]

This is not to minimize the important role mothers play in a child's life. Craig is calling attention to the harsh truth that boys growing up without fathers are much less likely to become responsible men in society—and everyone pays the price. The impact of a father and grandfather is disproportionate in its potential for harm or good compared to that of a mother or grandmother. In too many homes, mothers and grandmothers are expected to do the work God assigned to a man, and our boys pay the price as they enter adulthood.

My point is that when boys grow up without a father to teach and model what it means to be a man, it is not good. For whatever reason, there are far too many families without such a father. That is why I believe grandfathers are so vital. It is time for today's grandfathers to step to the plate and reject the misguided messages communicated to older men—messages like these:

1. **You've done your time, so step aside.** It may be unintentional, but I assure you the message is loud and clear that older men should stay out of the way. It's a young man's world. Do you believe you should stay out of the way? Is your time to make an impact over? If you believe this message, then you probably also believe that...

2. **You have nothing of value to offer.** Not only are we older men told "you've done your time", but we are also told we bring nothing of value to the table. The world has passed us by. We are out of touch and the past has nothing to contribute to the present or the future. This message, spawned by a focus on generational differences, idolizes youthfulness and marginalizes (or even demonizes) aging. Don't take the bait.

   Remember, Moses didn't start the most important work of his life until he was eighty. If you believe you have nothing of value to offer, I am here to say you are wrong. Job declared, "Is not wisdom found among the aged?" (Job 12:12) Old age does not necessarily translate into wisdom, but it should, which is why older men often succumb to this third lie…

3. **Retirement is the ultimate goal of life.** This view of retirement impacts the crisis of identity among older men. When we move away from the fact of our being created in the image and likeness of God, we toward empty pursuits and pleasures. In doing so, we automatically deform God's design for manhood.

    The world's retirement message encourages and promotes 'elder adolescence'—a life without purpose or meaningful identity beyond perpetual play. It's what I refer to in Chapter 5 as *elderitis*. Men caught in this affliction forget who they are.

    I wonder how different the impact of older saints would be if 'refirement' replaced 'retirement'. Refirement implies a greater purpose and new opportunities to make a difference later in life… like Caleb. It is a calling to men to take up a courageous, wholehearted devotion to God and His purposes. Will you dare to look in the mirror and ask yourself if you have the courage to man up and reject these wrong messages?

I hope you understand that **abdication** is an abomination to God. Abdication deprives your grandchildren of a rich spiritual example they desperately need. The Gospel does not give us license to run off to *Leisureville* or to sit on the sidelines. The power of the Gospel is in denying ourselves, taking up our cross and following Jesus with our whole being—for to me to live is Christ.

You can make a difference… if you choose to do so. If your grandchildren do not have a father in their home or a good father role model, you can be that model. I urge you to welcome that privilege and responsibility—for the sake of your grandsons and granddaughters. There is no higher calling for any man.

If you want to be the man God calls you to be, here are a few things to think about:

1. **Your worldview matters.** (I discussed this some in Chapter 13. I urge you to read it again.) George Barna says only 7% of all adults over 18 have a biblical worldview. Those of us in the generations of grandparents are only slightly ahead of the average at 9%.[3] Now translate that into men in those statistics, and grandfathers with a biblical worldview are mighty scarce.

    Even more unsettling is that, according to Barna, only 23% of all Americans who identify as "born again Christians" operate from a biblical worldview. If God's Word does not define your worldview, it is not a biblical worldview. A non-biblical worldview will lead to a distorted understanding of manhood and fatherhood (including grandfathers). In other words, you do what you believe.

2. **Your view of fatherhood/manhood matters.** When I use the term "father", I use it in the biblical sense of the word. Father does not refer only to the first-generation biological father we call Dad, but to all generations of living fathers in the bloodline or adopted line of a child. In other words, 'father' is an inclusive term that includes grandfathers, great grandfathers, and beyond.

    Fatherhood speaks to how all fathers in the family ancestry perform their roles. Fatherhood does not refer to specific roles, but qualities and marks of manhood that all biblical fathers share regardless of their role.

    Thus, fatherhood and manhood are interchangeable when referring to fathers. What manhood is does not change for men who are not fathers, except in applications specific to fathers. Mark Hancock believes "every call to manhood is a call to be a dad to a son—natural or not."[4] I agree. Even if a man is not a biological father, there is always a sense in which he is a 'spiritual father' to children in his faith communities. Therefore, *fatherhood* touches all men.

Second, my view of manhood is not shaped by public opinion or cultural values. It is determined by God's authority expressed in His Word. While certain cultural 'norms' influence our thinking and how we apply that thinking, only He who created male and female in His image has the authority to define how the two genders differ.

3. **Your view of the Gospel matters.** (See Chapter 2) Without a biblical worldview, your understanding of the Gospel will be skewed accordingly. Gentlemen, if the Gospel is nothing more to you than a future free pass to heaven with no relevance to your fatherhood, then your gospel is no gospel at all. The Gospel is not only about our salvation FROM our sin and God's judgment, but our call FOR living to the praise of His glory by making much of Christ is all we do.

Knowing the Gospel does not automatically mean you are changed by it. Jesus said, *"Not everyone who says to me, 'Lord, Lord', will enter the kingdom of heaven, but only he who does the will of my Father who is in heaven."* (Matthew 7:21) When the Gospel invades our heart and drives us, it changes everything. A profound and powerful new creation reality transforms our hearts and minds producing a life-giving legacy.

We will all leave a legacy, but a Gospel-shaped man leaves a legacy of Life (with a capital 'L'). As Craig Glass notes, an unintentional man only passes on a legacy of junk. "We had no say in determining our inheritance, but our legacy is ours to create. Our legacy moves outward from us. It is the impact and influence we pass on to others… that part of us that lives in other people and continues in them after we're gone."[5]

It might be profitable to pay attention to what God has to say about manhood and how it applies to grandfathers. To avoid any misunderstanding (and since many men don't read a great deal), God sent His own Son to this planet to show us what true manhood looks like. Jesus is the perfect model and example of manhood. Here are a few things he taught His disciples:

You know that those who are regarded as rulers of the Gentiles lord it over them, and their high officials exercise authority over them. Not so with you. Instead, whoever wants to become great among you must be your servant, and whoever wants to be first must be the slave of all. For even the Son of Man did not come to be served, but to serve, and to give His life as a ransom for many. (Mark 10-42-45)

Love the Lord, your God with all your heart and with all your soul and with your mind and will all your strength… and love your neighbor as yourself. There is no commandment greater than these. (Mark 12:30-31)

Why do you call me, 'Lord, Lord,' and do not do what I say? (Luke 6:46)

Watch out! Be on your guard against all kinds of greed; a man's life does not consist in the abundance of his possessions.… And do not set your heart on what you will eat or drink; do not worry about it. For the pagan world runs after all such things, and your Father knows that you need them. But seek His kingdom, and these things will be given to you as well. (Luke 12:15, 29-31)

The man who loves his life will lose it, while the man who hates his life in this world will keep it for eternal life. Whoever serves me must follow me; and where I am, my servant also will be. My Father will honor the one who serves me. (John 12:25-26)

Now that I, your Lord and Teacher, have washed your feet, you also should wash one another's feet. I have set you an example that you should do as I have done for you. (John 13:14-15)

The man of God lives his life according to what is right. Jesus came to reveal the truth and show us the Father from whom we get our understanding of what a father is.

Joaquin Molina writes in his book, *What is a Man?* how a true man lives his life:

> *The ultimate measure of a true man is not where he stands in*
> *ordinary moments of fun and entertainment, but where he*
> *stands at the crossroads of life when challenged by controversy*
> *of truth, standing up for what is right. The man who chooses to*

courageously act with strength of integrity in the face of difficult
situations and whose priority is to serve and protect the welfare
of his loved ones, defending his family against all potential harm,
is a true man. A true man will do anything it takes to leave
a legacy of blessing to his family. He wants to demonstrate his
capacity to protect his loved ones by always standing up for what
is right regardless what it may cost him to lose prestige, popularity,
fame, fortunes, or any such thing that could possibly compromise
the principles and convictions he holds true.[6]

Preparing for Adulthood

It bothers me that so many grandfathers miss how significant they are.
Lacking that understanding, they do not take up the battle for the hearts,
minds, and souls of their grandchildren. One contributing factor might be
that many men have no idea what it means to be a man of God, let alone
how to teach it to their sons or grandsons. There is no shortage of men whose
father or grandfather never taught them what it means to be a man.

If this describes you, I want to challenge you right now to believe you can
change that cycle in your family, You have the power to be a major influence
in preparing your grandchildren for adulthood. As a follower of Christ, God's
Word guarantees you already have **everything** *you need for life and godliness*
(2 Peter 1:3). Remember you are an heir of the Most High God, who speaks
to you with these words, "You are my son, whom I love." Believe what the
Father says, and then do what Jesus showed us a man does.

Remember, you cannot give what you do not have. If you want to grow in
your understanding of manhood and fatherhood so you can teach your own sons
and grandsons well, I also recommend you do four things. These are easy ways to
help you in this journey. We all need help and some prodding along the way.

1. Get involved in a good men's group that will help you grow as a man
    and provide the encouragement and friendships to help you teach
    another generation what it means to be a godly man.

2. Get a copy of *What is a Man?* by Joaquin Molina, and Noble Journey by Craig Glass, and study them. These books will guide you through the biblical teaching on manhood and how it applies to everyday life.

3. Go back and read chapters 9 and 10 on the spoken blessing. As a grandfather, I challenge you to man up and establish a practice of spoken blessing over each of your grandchildren. As you do, let them know you will be deliberately engaged in their lives in whatever way you possibly can because you care about them and believe God has a plan for their lives. Encourage them to pursue it.

4. Talk to your pastors about providing teaching on manhood and rite of passage from childhood to adulthood. I highly recommend Dr. Chuck Stecker with *A Chosen Generation*[7] to help any church do this. Many cultures in the world still practice rites of passage for men and women to mark their transition from childhood to adulthood. In the Western world, such rites, especially for boys, are rare. I think it's time to establish the rite of passage process in our families. I believe it will pay rich dividends as boys learn what it means to be men who treat women with respect and who model godly living. Grandfathers, you can hold the standard high for your family. Wave the flag of truth and march into battle for the hearts and souls of your families.

A Holy Dare

Here's what the apostle Paul wrote to the church at Philippi: *"Whatever you have learned or received or heard from me, or seen in me—put into practice."* (Philippians 4:9) That's an amazing statement, almost like a dare. *I dare you to find something in my life not worth imitating.* Would you say to your grandchildren, "Follow my example because everything I say and do is how you should also live"? That's a pretty courageous and audacious thing to say. But that is exactly what Paul is saying. *"Put into practice," he says, "**everything you see in me**"* (emphasis mine).

Is it realistic to live that kind of life? Not only is it realistic, it is imperative if we are going to show the next generations God's goodness, greatness, and glory. It is possible because of God's divine power through which we are partakers of Christ's life in us. Will we make mistakes? Without a doubt. But even those mistakes ought to be an example of how to demonstrate a fully mature life in Christ characterized by humility expressed through confession and forgiveness.

It's time to stop the cycle of irresponsibility. Grandfathers, you can make it right. Take your role seriously, and you will make a difference in showing your grandsons what it means to be a man. Do not abdicate this responsibility and hope someone else will step in the gap.

Even if your sons or sons-in-law are doing a great job, don't be a deadbeat grandfather. Get on your knees right now and ask God to show you how you can reinforce the process or supply what is missing. God will never ask you to do what He has not already equipped you to do.

A famous poem written by John Maxwell Edmonds has memorialized those who gave their lives fighting the enemies of our land in WWII. The last two lines read:

> *When you go home, Tell them of us and say,*
> *For your tomorrow, We gave our today.*[8]

Our sons and grandsons, daughters and granddaughters need men who give themselves so that they can have a tomorrow filled with hope, identity and meaning. These are the next generations of husbands and fathers, wives and mothers. What kind of legacy will we leave to them to build upon for another generation?

Courageous

The movie, *Courageous*, a Christian film produced by Sherwood Pictures, is a powerful story about responsible manhood. In the midst of tragedy and uncertainty, four men resolve to be the best fathers and husbands they can be according to God's plan. Out of one man's study and commitment, a Father's Resolution was developed and presented in a solemn ceremony with their families. They pledged to hold each other accountable to the terms of this resolution.

I encourage every grandfather to adopt this resolution. I urge you to find a band of grand-brothers who will stand with you in a pledge of accountability. Purchase a copy of *The Resolution for Men Study Guide.* In it you will find the Resolution and an opportunity to dig deep into what it means and how it impacts the way we live our lives. Use it as a framework for accountability with your band of courageous grand-brothers.

A Grandfather's Anthem

If there's a song that ought to be a Grandfather's Anthem across this land, it is John Mohr's song, *Find Us Faithful.* For me John's moving song, powerfully recorded by Steve Green, captures the essence of courageous, radical grandparenting in a broken world like ours. The chorus of John's song sums it up:

> *Oh may all who come behind us find us faithful*
> *May the fire of our devotion light their way.*
> *May the footprints that we leave*
> *Lead them to believe,*
> *And the lives we live inspire them to obey.*
> *Oh may all who come behind us find us faithful.*[9]

I had the privilege of serving with a man for twelve years on staff at a church in Denver. His name was Bob Frederich. He was the kind of man I wanted to emulate and was honored to serve beside. He was a passionate pastor and father, and I considered him a spiritual father.

At his memorial service, his grandchildren spoke about their grandfather. They had lots of fond memories to share, but the one thing they each declared was how much their grandfather "smelled like Jesus." Each grandchild spoke of how much their grandfather influenced them to want to know Jesus the way he did.

May the generations that follow behind us find us faithful. When asked who their heroes are, may our courageous faithfulness to Christ and the Gospel cause our children and grandchildren to declare, **"You are, because you smell like Jesus!"**

Courageous grandfathers seek above all to leave a lasting legacy of faith for those who come behind us. It is the legacy of grand-heroes who live poured out, planned out, and prayed out. May all who come behind us find us faithful—to the praise of His glory and for the salvation of all who will come after. Amen and amen!

Chapter Notes

Preface

1. *You Lost Me,* David Kinnaman, Barna Group-Baker Books, 2011, Kindle Books Loc. 485.

2. *Don't Waste Your Life,* Dr. John Piper, Crossway Books, 2003, pgs. 32-33.

Chapter 3

1. George Barna, *Faith & Community,* August 6, 2007

Chapter 4

1. *Only One Life,* a poem written by C.T. Stubbs, missionary to China, India and finally the African Congo, where he died at the age of seventy. He founded the Heart of Africa Mission, which later became known as WEC (World Evangelism Crusade) International. These familiar lines from his poem are just two lines from each stanza or verse of the original poem, which begins as follows:

> *Two little lines I heard one day*
> *Traveling along life's busy way,*
> *Bringing conviction to my heart*
> *And from my mind would not depart;*
> *Only one life twill soon be past,*
> *Only what's done for Christ will last.*

Chapter 6

See Appendix 6 for a list of good books and Family Time resources for grandparents

Chapter 8

1. Compiled from various accounts of Dr. Hendricks life, including an articles in the March issue of DTS Magazine after his memorial service, and books authored by Dr. Hendricks in which he told his story of his childhood.

Chapter 9

1. *The Blessing,* Gary Smalley and John Trent, Ph.D., Thomas Nelson Publishers, Nashville, TN, 1986, pg. 24.
    This is a read for every grandparent who wants to be a conduit of blessing in their family's life. Written in 1986 it is filled with practical tools and applications for establishing an environment of blessing in the home. We would do well to take to heart the teaching and practical suggestions offered in this book.

2. *Inappropriate touch:* Because touch is so central to our relationship, inappropriate touch is an abomination. It can irreparably devastate a life and relationship. True, the paranoia and fear that hangs over us should our touch be misunderstood can hinder us from reaching out appropriately. I understand the care we must exercise because of the profusion of perverts in our society. However, as is often the case, our overreactions have unleashed a new monster that seeks to hinder, if not dismantle, the relational needs we all have as image-bearers of God.

    The No Touch Monster is fed by suspicion and paranoia. Tragically, our physical withdrawals due to our fear that the No Touch Monster may be paroling around looking for someone to devour, only deprives another of that which is desperately needed. We must be wise and sensitive, but not paranoid. How do we discern the difference between appropriate and inappropriate touch?

    We start by taking a good look at ourselves. Appropriate, meaningful touch is motivated by a desire to bless someone with the most effective means possible. It is not concerned with the feelings of the one giving the blessing. The person who is looking for a pleasurable experience is walking down a dangerous, destructive path. If it is ever about you, it will probably be inappropriate. This requires some honest self-examination. We also need to make ourselves accountable to others. It is not hard to pick up on red flags in those who are disingenuous.

Appropriate touch, on the other hand (no pun intended), can be something as simple as a hand on the shoulder or head, or even a gentle touch on the arm. In the right situations a hug or a kiss may be appropriate expressions of love and value. Always ask, *Will this be meaningful and provide the most positive response possible for the one I wish to bless? How will the person I want to bless most likely respond to this expression of love and affection?*

Careless expressions of touch rooted in self-gratifying motivations turn an opportunity to bless into a curse, even if it was unintentional. Our responsibility is to guard our heart and make sure we know what is appropriate in any situation. The way in which we reach out to a small child might not be appropriate for a young teen, especially someone of the opposite sex. How a man reaches out to a young woman, even if she is a granddaughter, may be very different from how another woman may embrace that same young woman.

Chapter 11

1. *Well-Versed Living* by Caroline Boykin; *Significant Living*, September 2011 issue.
2. *The Well-Versed Family: Raising Kids of Faith Through (Do-Able!) Scripture Memory* by Caroline Boykin, Tate Publishing, 2007, web site: www.wellversedliving.com.

3. *Passing On A Written Legacy* by Lana Rockwell. Lana provides some very practical ways to recall much of your life story and write it down so that your family will have a first-person perspective on the family history. Lana's web site is: www.mymemoriesforyou.net

4. My Hope to You, www.mh2u.org, by Merlin and Theresa Buhl, is a great site with tools to help you write your story and print it in an attraction bound book.

5. *Legacy Journal,* by Cavin Harper. Available on the Christian Grandparenting website store in a downloadable pdf file you can print at home, complete and then print as many copies as you want for your grandchildren.

Chapter 12

1. *The Ultimate Gift,* Jim Stovall, David C. Cook, Colorado Springs, CO, 2001, pgs. 146 and 151. Also available in a movie version. Either the book or the movie would be an excellent resource to use with your grandchildren followed by a discussion about those things in life that really matter. A study guide is also available to work through with your children/grandchildren. For more information about this book, DVD and other resources, visit the web site at www.theultimategift.com.

2. *How Should We Then Live? The Rise and Decline of Western Thought and Culture,* Francis Schaeffer, Crossway Books, Wheaton, IL, 1976.

    Francis Schaeffer, theologian, author, philosopher, pastor and found of L'Abri communties in Switzerland, wrote a number of works dealing with cultural issues and the arts with the eye of a Christian apologists. His two major works were *A Christian Manifesto* and *What Ever Happened To The Human Race* (also a film series) dealt with the problem of secular humanism in which man is the measure of all things, not God and the Word. Another of his works, also made into a film documentary, was *How Should We Then Live? The Rise and Decline of Western Thought and Culture.* In this work he traces western history from the time of ancient Rome to the mid-1970's and the changing patterns of thought the developed throughout these periods. He warned of the destructive consequences of building a society on humanism, which ultimately produces relativism and no way to distinguish right from wrong. He purpose was to challenge society to consider the ultimate consequences of basing a society on humanism rather than the absolute truth of God's Word and an infinite, personal God. He foresaw the cultural changes that now pervade our time. While his warnings were greatly discussed in churches and student groups across the land, his warnings still went largely unheeded.

3. *The Ultimate Living Will Workbook,* Cavin T. Harper; available through the Christian Grandparenting Network website beginning March 2019.

Chapter 13

1. *Culture Making: Recovering Our Creative Calling,* Andy Crouch, IVP Books, 2009.
2. Ibid., pg. 69.
3. *Taste and See: Savoring the Supremacy of God in All of Life* by John Piper (Multnomah Press, 2005), pg. 300-301.
4. *The Meaning Of Marriage: Facing The Complexities of Commitment With The Wisdom of God,* by Timothy Keller, founding pastor of Redeemer Presbyterian Church in New York City; 2011.

Americans have not taken divorce seriously, especially as it impacts our children caught in the web of divorce. Here are some *Shocking Statistics About Children and Divorce* by Larry Bilotta, Marriage Success Secrets, www.marriage-success-secrets.com; various sources are cited in this blog for each of the statistics listed. See his web site for the sources. These are things our adult children need to know, and we need to be discussing with our teen grandchildren as they begin thinking about opposite sex relationships in dating and marriage.

Consider some samplings of the damage caused to our children by the divorce-as-a-way-of-life mentality in our society:

- Half of all American children will witness the breakup of a parent's marriage. Of these, nearly half will also see the breakup of a parent's second marriage.
- Forty percent of children growing up in America are being raised without their father.
- Studies in the early 1980s show that children in repeat divorces earned lower grades and their peers rated them as less pleasant to be around.
- Compared to children from homes disrupted by death, children from divorced homes have more psychological problems.
- Children living with both biological parents are 20-35 percent more physically healthy than other children from broken homes.
- Seventy percent of long-term prison inmates grew up in broken homes.
- Children and adults from broken homes are nearly twice as likely to attempt suicide than those who do not come from broken homes.

5. *Preparing Children for Marriage,* Dr. Josh Mulvihill, P&R Publishing, 2017.
6. *The Changing Profile of Unmarried Parents* by Gretchen Livingston, Pew Research Center Social and Demographic Trends, April 25, 2018.
7. *The Spiral of Silence: Public Opinion—Our Social Skin,* Elisabeth Noelle-Neumann, 1993, University of Chicago Press.

The spiral of silence is the theory that a person is less likely to voice an opinion on a topic if one feels that one is in the minority for fear of reprisal or isolation from the majority. It begins with fear of reprisal or isolation, and escalates from there. The fear of isolation is the centrifugal force that accelerates the spiral of silence. Noelle-Neuman suggests demonstrates how mass media play a large part in determining what the dominant opinion is due to the fact that our direct observation of issues is limited to a small percentage of the population. The mass media have an enormous impact on how public opinion is portrayed, and can dramatically impact an individual's perception about where public opinion lies, whether or not that portrayal is factual. Noelle-Neumann describes the spiral of silence as a dynamic process, in which predictions about public opinion become fact as mass media's coverage of the minority opinion becomes the status quo, and the majority becomes less likely to speak out. We see this carried out in the political correct arenas of morality and social justice. Intimidation, when a minority opinion is imposed upon a larger majority through fear of reprisal or unmerited accusations, becomes a primary means of silencing the majority opinion and compelling it to adopt what it might otherwise reject.

Crucial points to the theory

- People have a fear of being rejected by those in their social environment, which is called "fear of isolation."
- People are constantly observing the behaviors of those around them, and seeing which gain approval and disapproval from society.
- People unconsciously issue their own threats of isolation by showing signals of approval or disapproval.
- Threats of isolation are avoided by a person's tendency to refrain from making a statement about something they think might attract objections.
- People are more willing to publicly state things that they believe will be accepted positively.
- The spiral effect begins because when people who are seen as

representing majority opinion, often authority figures, speak out confidently. The opposition feels a greater sense of fear of isolation and is further convinced to remain silent, since they perceive themselves to be in the minority. The feelings continue to grow in either direction exponentially.

- A strong moral component is necessary for the issue to activate the spiral.
- If there is a social consensus, the spiral will not be activated. There must be two opposing forces.
- The mass media has a strong influence on this process.
- Fear and threat of isolation are subconscious processes.
- The spiral of silence only "holds a sway" over the public for a limited time.
- If a topic activates the spiral of silence, this means that the issue is a great threat to social cohesion.

8. "Defining Marriage Down", by Adam Mersereau, Touchstone: A Journal of Mere Christianity; November 2003
   Note: The subject of same-sex marriage is gaining momentum in our country, and if allowed to continue as it is, it will have devastating repercussion upon the traditional family in America. It behooves us all to equip ourselves well for the discussions (if permitted) that will need to be engaged. T. M. Moore and the Colson Center have prepared some very useful and information resources and activities for engaging in this conversation. I have listed these in the Appendix. I urge you to read up, wise up and be proactive about seeking opportunities to compassionately and graciously engage in dialogue with your families and grandchildren.

9. "I'm Gay and I Oppose Same-Sex Marriage", by Doug Mainwaring, *Public Discourse,* March 8, 2013.

10. *More Americans Tailoring Religion to Fit Their Needs,* by Cathy Lynn Grossman, USA Today, September 14, 2011.

Chapter 14

1. *Place and Placelessness in America: The New Meaning of Mobility;* Christine Rosen, The New Atlantis: A Journal of Technology and Society, Number 31, Spring 2011, pp. 40-46.

2. *God's Technology: Training Our Children to Use Technology to God's Glory,* Dr. David Murray, www.HeadHeartHand.org, Puritan Reformed Theological Seminary. A free study guide is available with the DVD.

Chapter 15

1. *Amusing Ourselves to Death: Public Discourse in the Age of Show Business,* Neil Postman, Penguin Books, 1985, pg.xix.

2. *Growing Up Digital—Wired for Distraction;* Matt Richtel, The New York Times, November 21, 2010.

3. *Amusing Ourselves to Death: Public Discourse in the Age of Show Business,* Neil Postman, Penguin Books, 1985, pg.xx.

4. Prince EA YouTube: *Can We Auto-Correct Humanity?* Link: https://www.youtube.com/watch?v=dR18EIhrQjQ

5. *Is True Friendship Dying Away?*, Mark Vernon, USA Today, July 26, 2010.

6. *Myth: A Little TV Never Hurt Anybody,* Bill Bumpus, OneNewsNow article based upon an interview with Melissa Henson of the Parents Television Council, May 5, 2010; Research data from a study published in the Archives of Pediatrics and Adolescent Medicine.

7. *Generation M2: Media In The Lives of 8- To 18-Year-Olds;* A Kaiser Family Foundation Study, January 2010.

8. *Predator Statistics,* InternetSafety101.org web site, Enough Is Enough, a ministry of Youth For Christ to make the internet safer for children and families; research data provided by the Crimes Against Children Research Center. A great deal of valuable information is available through the Enough Is Enough web site that would useful to both parents and grandparents. www.enough.org or www.internetsafety101.org.

Chapter 16

1. *Dual Commissions: Evangelizing and Engaging Culture,* Chuck Colson, Breakpoint, November 30, 2011. www.colsoncenter.org

Chapter 17

1. *The False Enforcement of Unpopular Norms,* Willer, Kuwabara, and Macy, University of California, Berkeley. An informative study in the reasons and influences behind the enforcement of group consensus and unpopular norms that violate individual private beliefs. Jim Jones and the Jonestown Massacre is one example of how masses can be persuaded and convinced by charismatic leaders to do the most extreme actions and adopt extreme beliefs not otherwise held. In fact, not only do individuals comply to such extreme norms, but they enforce others to do so as well. The study suggests that people become trapped in a "self-enforcing equilibrium in which they pressure one another in order to cover up their own private doubts", and this may appear genuine to casual observers and even researchers if they do not understand the reality of "false enforcement".

2. *Don't Waste Your Life,* John Piper, Crossway Books, Wheaton, IL, 2003, page 32. One of Piper's best books on practical Christian living. The big idea of this book is living lives that display the glory and greatness of God in all we do. It involves risk, suffering, mission, mercy and joy because Christ is our treasure.

   Piper's teaching from God's Word is right on the money for grandparents who take their roles seriously and do not buy into the retirement myth. And as John Piper notes, risk taking involves living our lives in such a way that we "show he [Jesus] is more precious than life…if we walk away from risk to keep ourselves safe and solvent, we will waste our lives". This is a book every grandparent (and every believer) should read. Piper's perspective on new birth and the resultant life that makes Christ look great—that He is our "all-satisfying treasure"—is at the heart of the Gospel and what it means to not waste our lives. If we do, an entire generation could grow up not knowing the Lord and truth that can set them free to be all God created us to be.

3. Dr. Haddon Robinson, Gordon Conwell Seminary. I can't locate the exact source of when and where Dr. Robinson made this comment, but I do have it in my personal notes from a speech he delivered several years ago. I just don't remember where.

4. *Grandparenting with a Purpose: Effective Ways to Pray for Your Grandchildren,* Lillian Ann Penner, Crossbooks, A Division of Lifeway, 2010. Copies can also be ordered from www. GrandparentingWithAPurpose.com

5. Dr. Mark Young, "Charitable Orthodoxy", Denver Seminary Magazine, Summer 2011, pg. 2.

Chapter 18

1. *Reviving Fatherhood,* Viewpoint by Mark Earley, January 14, 2010, www. breakpoint.org

2. *Noble Journey: The Quest for a Lasting Legacy* by Craig M. Glass, Peregrine Ministries, 2017, pg. 19-20.

3. Dr. George Barna, *A Biblical Worldview is Shockingly Uncommon Among Important Segment of the US,* Source: Metaformation Inc., 2018

4. *Dads and Sons;* talk by Mark Hancock at the 2018 Fatherhood CoMission; Mark T. Hancock, CEO of Trail Life USA

5. Glass, *Noble Journey,* pg. 127

6. What is a Man? By Dr. Joaquin G. Molina, Springs of Life Media, Miami, FL, 2013, pg. 11 (www.whatisaman.com)

7. A Chosen Generation; Dr. Chuck Stecker, Founder and President; www.achosengeneration.info. Dr. Stecker offers a powerful childhood to adulthood seminar entitled "Men of Honor/Women of Virtue" for every generation in the local church. It culminates with a powerful, life-changing rites of passage ceremony with the whole congregation.

8. The Kohima Epitaph, The Burma Star Association, www.burmastar.org.
   uk. The text of these words used on several war memorials come from
   a poem written by John Maxwell Edmonds (1875 -1958), an English
   Classicist, who had put them together among a collection of 12 epitaphs
   for WWI in 1916.

9. *Find Us Faithful,* music and lyrics by John Mohr, 1987; copyright Gaither
   Music Company, 1703 S Park AvenueAlexandria, IN 46001-8063. Used
   by permission.

Appendix 1

Technology Resources

1. *Flickering Pixels: How Technology Shapes Your Faith,* Shane Hipps, Zondervan Publishing, 2009.
2. *Screens and Teens: Connecting with our Kids in a Wireless Age,* Kathy Koch, PhD., Moody Publishers, 2015.
3. Tricia Goyer, "Parents in a Digital World", Parent Edition of April 2007 issue of Focus on the Family magazine. Available online at www.focusonthefamily.com/parenting
4. *Character in a Tech-Overloaded World,* by Linda Keffer, Helping Families Thrive web site at Focus on the Family. Available online at www.focusonthefamily.com/parenting
5. AXIS Ministries; www.axis.org; Provide numerous resources for parents and grandparents to help us understand what is going on in the tech world, and especially social media. They provide Parents Guides, Conversation Kits and daily newsletter called Cultural Translator. Worth checking out.
6. *Plugged In (www.pluggedin.com);* an online publication of Focus On The Family designed to shine a light on the world of popular entertainment while giving families the essential tools they need to understand, navigate and impact the culture in which they live. Through reviews, articles and discussions, the goal is to "spark intellectual thought, spiritual growth and a desire to follow the command of Colossians 2:8: 'See to it that no one takes you captive through hollow and deceptive philosophy, which depends on human tradition and the basic principles of this world rather than on Christ.'" This is a valuable resource for families in a number of media technology arenas, including movies, video games, TV, music, etc.

7. *Pew Internet (www.pewinternet.org)*; a project of the Pew Research Center; a nonpartisan, nonprofit "fact tank" that provides information on the issues, attitudes and trends shaping America and the world. The Project produces reports exploring the impact of the internet on families, communities, work and home, daily life, etc. Web site:

8. *Wired Safety (www.wiredsafety.org)*; provides one-to-one help, extensive resources, information, and education to people of all ages on a myriad of Internet, mobile, gaming and interactive technology safety issues. Web site:

9. *Common Sense Media (www.commonsense.org)*; Common Sense Media is dedicated to improving the lives of kids and families by providing the trustworthy information, education, and independent voice they need to thrive in a world of media and technology.

10. *The Dumbest Generation: How the Digital Age Stupifies Young Americans and Jeopardizes Our Future,* Mark Bauerlein, published by the Penguin Group, 2008. While I don't care for the title of this book, it is a good insight into how the digital age has contributed to the 'dumbing down' of many of our youth.

11. *Amusing Ourselves to Death: Public Discourse in the Age of Show Business,* Neil Postman, Penguin Books, 1985. This is an important work written before the digital age exploded on the scene. Postman's insights into how the movement toward electronic media and entertainment has negatively impacted our minds and societal values is a prophetic work for our day. I think it is a good read for grandparents to understand the world we helped create.

PLAN A TECH-FAST:

As with all the good things, there are downsides as well. In spite of the benefits we enjoy with all the technology available to us today, diligence will increase our awareness of the threat technology can make to authentic human relationships. We can be in the same room together, and still be completely isolated from one another. Obsessions with social networking, texting, online games, and the growing use of portable devices like smartphones, tablets, and mobile game devices, make it easy to avoid meaningful relational engagement—having conversations.

At the same time, technology has increased our ability to connect with people anywhere in the world like never before. This is a huge benefit for those wanting to stay connected even though we are separated by vast oceans, or a few states. The convenience of cell phone connectivity has made some aspects of life better and safer. Unfortunately, the flip-side of this great blessing is what I call *technobesity*. We are growing fat, relationally disconnected, and overloaded with useless information in the world of cyberspace. What can we do to counter this trend toward 'technobesity'?

I suggest we try a 'tech-fast' for a period. A food fast from time to time helps to cleanse our physical bodies of toxins. When combined with prayer, it is a spiritual cleansing as well. So, why not do a 'tech-fast' from time to time? It can be for a day, two days, a week, or whatever period of time you choose. You could declare a 'tech-fast' for just a few hours when family comes to visit.

Here are some suggestions to make your tech-fast profitable and beneficial for all. If you just can't do it all, then you may have a serious case of *technobesity* that may warrant some more drastic measures. F. B. Meyer wrote, "We never test the resources of God until we attempt the impossible." At a time when our lives are consumed with technology, it might seem like an impossible task. Just give it a try. Here are some ideas for implementing a tech-fast. See if it doesn't make a difference in your own family.

1. Sit down with family members and discuss the idea. Why are you doing it? What do you hope to accomplish? What are the benefits? How long will the fast period be? If you get the nod to move ahead, work together to plan how the time will be spent. (Remember, if you just fast from technology, but plan nothing to replace it, you are really planning to fail.)

2. Agree to turn off and NOT USE your TV, iPhone (or Smartphone), iPad, tablets or computers. No iPods or ear buds allowed. That means you will not be checking email or Facebook or Twitter during the period of the fast.

3. Here are some ways to use your time during the tech-fast:
    a. Pray
    b. Sit down and talk. Talk about life experiences currently going on, social issues, or family history. Ask questions that require more than 'yes' or 'no' answers.
    c. Play some table games
    d. Talk a walk or go to the park and toss a frisby or ball
    e. Do a Bible study together.
    f. Do a craft project

4. Conclude the tech-fast period by speaking a personal blessing over each member of your family—spouse, grandchildren, children, etc.

5. Debrief: briefly evaluate what you experienced. What did your learn? What were the challenges? Can you do it again? What would you do differently?

Author's Note: I'd like to hear from you about your personal experience with doing a tech-fast. Send me an email at *charper@christiangrandparenting.net* and tell me how it went.

One more thought: consider a limited fast in which all cell phones, computers, game devices, iPods and television programs are off-limits, but allow watching a selected movie (like *Courageous* or *October Baby*), or a teaching DVD (*such as Doing the Right Thing*) followed by an interaction time with your family or friends.

Appendix 2

FAMILY DISCIPLESHIP

I've assembled a list of several resources I think are good for grandparents to have in the resource tool box for teaching and discussing important topics that have to do with building a biblical worldview and evaluating how to know whether things your grandchildren hear or learn are true. There are so many more than I have listed here, but these are my top choices that I recommend to almost any grandparent.

Early Childhood/ Grade School/Teens

1. *Six Ways to Help Children Live According to God's Word* by Josh Mulvihill, downloadable e-book; available only at www.gospelshapedfamily,com/store
2. *Family Discipleship Toolkit,* Josh Mulvihill, free download with tons of tools for parents and grandparents; www.gospelshapedfamily.com/store
3. *Talking with Your Kids About God: 30 Conversations Every Christian Parent Must Have,* Natasha Crain, Baker Books, 2017. Natasha' book is written for parents, but as a grandparent I found it extremely helpful in having conversations about tough topics with my grandchildren. It is especially useful for older grade school age and teens.
4. *The Story of Reality* by Gregory Koukl, Zondervan, 2017.
5. *Family Time Training,* Kurt Weaver and Jenna Hallock; their web site offers a huge palette of resource activities including a special section of activities especially planned for grandparents to use with their grandchildren. www.famtime.com.

For Your Own Learning

1. *Tactics: A Game Plan for Discussing Your Christian Convictions* by Gregory Koukl, Zondervan, 2009.

2. *A Practical Guide to Culture: Helping the Next Generation Navigate Today's World* by John Stonestreet and Brett Kunkle, David C. Cook, 2017. This is certainly a more involved read, though easy to read and understand. Lots of practical discussion questions and action steps for each chapter. If you want to know whether your worldview lines up with Scripture, this would be an excellent resource.

3. *Biblical Grandparenting: Exploring God's Design for Disciple-Making and Passing Faith to Future Generations,* Dr. Josh Mulvihill, Bethany House, 2018.

4. *Soul Nourishment: Satisfying Our Deep Longing for God,* Deborah Haddix, Warner Press, 2018.

5. *The Treasure Principle,* by Randy Alcorn; pg. 19-20. Randy unpacks the secret of giving according to the radical teaching of Jesus. This little book is full of powerful truths that will change your life and the lives of your children/grandchildren if your embrace them.

Appendix 3

14-DAY SPIRITUAL JOURNEY
Preparing to Implement *The Ultimate Living Will* Plan

This 14-day spiritual journey is an adventure in trust and faith. You are choosing to act upon God's promises in response to His commands to bless others with the various assets He has given you. This is not necessarily a comfortable or easy journey to take. If you have a tight hold on that which you have, material or otherwise, or if you have trouble acknowledging how much God has given to you for His purposes, you will find this journey difficult, if not impossible, to continue. On the other hand, if you persevere by faith, I believe you will see God work in ways you may never have dreamed possible.

Remember Jesus' words that your life does not consist in "the abundance of your possessions" (Luke 12:13-21), and that he who would "whoever loses his life for my sake will find it" (Matthew 10:37-39). Proverbs 11:25 describes the generous man, not only as one who prospers, but who is himself refreshed as he refreshes others. The life lived well is a generous and fulfilling life. My prayer is that you will discover the joy of this truth through this spiritual journey and pass this on through your legacy to the next generations.

Here are some daily guides from God's Word to keep you focused on the good way where God promises rest for your soul and refreshing for others—especially your family. Meditate on these Scriptures. Let them transform your mind and heart, and serve as a call to action by faith. Let the Spirit of God teach you and work in you for the Father's purposes. In this spirit, then,

I pray that "God will fill you with the knowledge of His will through all spiritual wisdom and understanding… that you may live a life worthy of the Lord and may please Him in every good work, growing in the knowledge of God." (Colossians. 19-10). May He use you and all that He has given you to bless those He desires to bless through you.

Let the adventure begin!

14-DAY SPIRITUAL JOURNEY PLAN

DAY 1:

> **Scripture:** Matthew 19:16-22
>
> **Action Point:** If you are a person of means and great wealth, this passage is especially difficult. Generosity is always a matter of the heart. Ask God to search your heart and expose anything that may be hindering you from opening your hand to God's purposes for what He has given you.

DAY 2:

> **Scripture:** Jeremiah 9:23-24
>
> **Action Point:** Once more ask the Lord to reveal any points of pride or unwillingness to surrender all He given for His purposes. Take time today to focus on God's goodness and all that He has done for you so that we will not boast in anything but Him and His grace.

DAY 3:

> **Scripture:** Matthew 25:14-15
>
> **Action Point:** Sit down and make an inventory of all the material assets God has given to you. It may be a lot; it may be a little. The point is to acknowledge what God has provided. When you

finish your inventory, thank God for what He has provided and acknowledge His ownership.

DAY 4:

Scripture: Acts 3:6

Action Point: Material assets are not all the assets God has given us to spend and dispose of for the blessing of others. Take time today and tomorrow to make an inventory of those non-material assets with which God has blessed you (education, spiritual gifts, knowledge, skill sets, life lessons, relationships, personality, family, faith, etc.)

DAY 5:

Scripture: Matthew 25: 16-30

Action Point: Look over the inventory of assets God has blessed you with. Now ask Him to give you wisdom to understand how He would have you spend, invest or dispose of these assets to bless others. Ask how these assets could be used to bless others. If you have hoarded these assets for yourself, confess that now. With a repentant heart ask for forgiveness, and then offer them with open hand and heart for His purposes.

DAY 6:

Scripture: Ephesians 2:10

Action Point: God has already prepared you and those who will receive the blessings from your hand. Prayerfully make a list of people (family and others) you know God would want use you to bless with these assets He has given you. Pray over each name on the list and ask God to show you how He wants you to invest in each person.

DAY 7:

Scripture: Colossians 3:17

Action Point: Now that you have identified a list of people the Lord wants you to bless as you spend, invest or otherwise dispose of the assets He has given you, ask Him for clear understanding about how best to do that? There may a situation in which you don't know the answer to who, when or where, only what. Simply wait upon the Lord and ask Him to lead you to the individual or individuals He wants to bless through you and give glory to Him.

DAY 8:

Scriptures: 2 Corinthians 8:12; Mark 12:41-44

Action Point: Continue to ask God for wisdom, courage and alertness to His leading. Guard against doubt or the notion that you have nothing to give. Even if you have little materially, the Lord has given you exactly what is needed to bless others, including your family. The poor widow reminds us that it is not the size of the gift or what kind of gift is offered but the willing, worshiping heart of the giver that God will bless.

DAY 9:

Scripture: I Timothy 6:18-19

Action Point: Continuing praying for the people whom God will be sending to you and identifying to you for blessing and meeting a need. Guard your heart so that you are always cheerfully and happily serving those He sends to you, regardless of how they might respond.

DAY 10:

Scripture: 2 Corinthians 9:8, 11

Action Point: What has God revealed to you thus far about your own heart and the needs of those around you? Are there lessons and blessings you have received you want to thank God for and share with others?

DAY 11:

> **Scripture:** Luke 12:15-21
>
> **Action Point:** You may have begun to discover some of the rare treasures God has entrusted to you to use for His glory. In contrast to the rich farmer in this parable, what have you learned about what it means to live a life that is rich towards God? How can you truly worship Him and live Life (with a capital 'L')—a life that demonstrates what it means to be rich towards God?

DAY 12:

> **Scriptures:** Matthew 6:19-21; Romans 12:1-8
>
> **Action Point:** Each day from here on out ask the Lord to show you how He wants you to bless another through the assets He has provided. Thank Him for the special blessings He will reveal to you and through you each day.

DAY 13:

> **Scripture:** Philippians 4:-11-12
>
> **Action Point:** What have I learned about contentment in these last few weeks? How will my life be different as a result?

DAY 14:

> **Scripture:** 2 Corinthians 5:10
>
> **Action Point:** In light of God's warning about being judged according to the way your life was lived, how does this impact the way you see your life? What have you learned throughout this 14-Day Adventure with God that may change how you use your assets? How could you share what you have learned with others?

Appendix 4

THE BLESSING

I. GENERAL BLESSING

The general or recurring blessing (you may choose to do it daily, weekly or monthly) is a powerful tool for helping our children and grandchildren know, love and follow Christ with their all their heart. Through the laying on of hands and the spoken words of blessing, we become conduits for a consistent, deliberate encounter with God's transforming power and favor, and a wall of protection in which they will experience a sense of security in God.

Here are steps that will help you in the establishment of a Recurring Family Blessing for each of your children/grandchildren…

1. If the children are old enough, explain to them what you want to do with the blessing and why.
2. Hold them or touch them in a sincere and meaningful way when you say the blessing over them, laying one hand on their head as a symbol of your being an instrument through which God blesses.
3. Pick a time and frequency and stick with it. It can be daily, weekly, or whenever you have them over to your house, but the key is consistency.
4. Choose the blessing you will say. It can be the same blessing every time, or you can vary the blessing from time to time. (See examples below)
5. JUST DO IT!!! It is never too late to start, but it is always too soon to delay.

EXAMPLES OF BLESSINGS FROM SCRIPTURE:

And the LORD spoke to Moses, saying: "Speak to Aaron and his sons, saying, 'This is the way you shall bless the children of Israel. Say to them: "The LORD bless you and keep you; The LORD make His face shine upon you, And be gracious to you; The LORD lift up His countenance upon you, And give you peace." ' "So they shall put My name on the children of Israel, and I will bless them." Numbers 6:22-27 NKJV

1. As Aaron spoke God's blessing over the people of Israel, so I speak God's blessing over my children/grandchildren today.

    _________, may the Lord bless you and keep you; may the Lord make His face to shine upon you and be gracious unto you; may the Lord turn His face toward you and give you peace in the name of Jesus Christ our Lord.

2. Ephesians 3:17-19

    _________, I pray that you, being rooted and established in love, may have power together with all the saints to grasp how wide and long and high and deep is the love of Christ, and to know this love that surpasses knowledge, that you may be filled to the measure of all the fullness of God, in Jesus' name.

3. 2 Thessalonians 2:16-17

    _________, may our Lord Jesus Christ Himself and God the Father, who loved us and by His grace gave us eternal encouragement and good hope, encourage your heart and strengthen you in every good deed and word, in the name of the Father, Son and Holy Spirit.

4. Romans 15:13

    _________, may the God of hope fill you with all joy and peace as you trust in Him, so that you may overflow with hope by the power of the Holy Spirit, in the name of the Father, Son and Holy Spirit.

5. May the Lord bless you with His favor and kindness; may He keep
    you by His power and strength, and deliver them from all evil; may
    His face shine upon you with the light of His radiant love; may you
    delight in the abundant riches of God's amazing grace; may the Lord
    make His face to smile on you; may He shield your heart and mind
    with His truth and abiding peace, His perfect peace that passes all
    understanding.

II. THE PERSONAL BLESSING

Few things can be as powerful and meaningful in your child/grandchild's
life than a personal, spoken blessing at specific 'milestones' in their life.
The pronouncement of blessing has been a part of family life among
God's people from the earliest days. Prayerfully consider what God would
have you speak into the life of your children that would encourage them
and build them up in Christ, then write it out on the page provided.
Make it your own and let it speak truth and life into your child/
grandchild. A blessing should include the following…

1. An Affirmation of High Value
    Communicate to your child/grandchild that they are something
    special, and that you value them highly. Identify a particular trait
    you wish to emphasize and express how you value that trait. Word
    pictures can be a powerful way to express that value.

2. A Picture of a Special Future
    This is a reflection of how well you know your child/grandchild
    and the gifts and interests he/she has already developed. The idea
    is to express an expectation of success and accomplishment, not for

worldly gain, but according to that which God has already purposed for them. You are saying, "I believe in you and expect you to succeed in that which God has prepared in advance for you."

3. An Active Commitment
It great to speak blessing to our children and grandchildren, but now we must demonstrate our willingness to stand with them and walk them in the journey ahead. Inconsistency and lack of follow through will tend to negate any positive reinforcement you may communicate verbally.

NOTE: Be brief and to the point. Don't worry about all the details of someone's life or another's example. Capture the essence of what you want to say and say it so they will remember it. On the next few pages you will find some examples to help you write your own.

EXAMPLES

A Grandparents' Blessing
For Our Grandson

_______________ ___________

_______________,

While you were yet in your mother's womb, the blessings had already begun in your Grandma's and my heart.

_______________, your presence has brought us all joy as we have watched you grow, taken your first steps, and spoken your first words. Your hurts have been our hurts, and we shared in your laughter.

_______________, your accepting Jesus Christ into your heart and life was an answer to daily prayer. Our prayers for you now are for God's watchful care over you. May He protect you during these young years, and may you grow up physically, mentally, and spiritually strong. Whatever you choose to do in life, may you always be God's man, and let the light within you shine before family and other people.

_______________, with thanksgiving in our hearts, we are thankful to God for being allowed to be part of your life.

Grandma and Grandpa _______________

A Grandparents' Blessing for

____

_______________, you are such a blessing to grandpa and grandma. A verse that we found for you is Ephesians 4:32 – *"Be kind and compassionate to one another forgiving each other just as in Christ, God forgave you."*

_______________, the Lord is giving you many opportunities to be kind, compassionate, and forgiving to those around you at dance classes, at school, and with your family and friends.   Though given originally to Israel, we believe the promise of God in Jeremiah 29:11-13 is for you as well, and so we've inserted your name in this passage. It says,

> *"For I know the plans I have for _________ declares the Lord,*
> *plans to prosper her and not to harm her, plans to give her hope*
> *and a future. Then ___________ will call upon me and I will*
> *listen to her. ____________ will seek me and find me when she*
> *seeks me with all her heart."*

Our prayer is that for all of your life you will **call** upon the Lord in prayer, that you will **seek** Him in His Word, because there you will ***find*** Him.

______________, you are very intuitive and our prayer is that you will use your intuition to discern when and how to show kindness, compassion and forgiveness to others.

We enjoy spending time with you, doing things you like to do, enjoy watching you as you grow up - what a blessing you are to us! We pray that you will continue to be a blessing to others as well.

You are our granddaughter, precious to us, and we love you.

Grandpa & Grandma ______________________________

Appendix 5

ADDITIONAL RESOURCES

1. *Don't Bite Your Tongue: How To Foster Rewarding Relationships With Your Adult Children* by Ruth Nemzoff; St. Martin's Press, New York, NY; 2008. Ruth has written a valuable book about building rewarding relationships with your adult children. While not written from a biblical or Christian perspective, she provides wonderful anecdotes and insights into managing a positive relationship without a trite one-size-fits-all approach that many writers take. It provides a very helpful perspective for grandparents.

2. *Setting Boundaries with Your Adult Children: Six Steps to Hope and Healing for Struggling Parents* by Allison Bottke; Harvest House Publishers, Eugene, OR; 2008. Another very helpful book for those dealing with extremely difficult situations because of painful choices their adult children make. Allison writes from a biblical point of view about tough love issues. If you are engaged in heart-wrenching situations with your adult children, you should consider reading this book.

3. *Grand Parenting: Strengthening Your Family and Passing on Your Faith* by Josh Mulvihill, Bethany House, Bloomington, MN, 2018.

4. *Passing the Legacy: 7 Keys for Grandparents Making a Difference* by Catherine Jacobs, Elm Hill/Harper Collins Christian Publishing, Nashville, TN, 2018.

5. *Grandparenting with a Purpose: Effective Ways to Pray for Your Grandchildren* by Lillian Penner. Lillian is the National Prayer Coordinator of the Christian Grandparenting Network. Develop your prayer life as you pray for your family, and especially your grandchildren.

You'll find practical examples of prayer to help you get started, and creative ways to make your prayers more meaningful and effective. [Available at the CGN store: www.christiangrandparenting.net or from Lillian's site at www.grandparentingwithapurpose.com]

6. *The H.E.A.R.T. of Grandparenting: 5 Keys to Being the Best Grandparent Possible,* Dr. Ken Canfield, Dayspring, 2018.

7. *Never Too Late: Encouraging Faith in Your Adult Child,* Rob Rienow, Kregel Publications, Grand Rapids, MI, 2011

8. *Men of Honor, Women of Virtue: The Power of Rites of Passage into Godly Adulthood,* Dr. Chuck Stecker, Siesmic Publishing Group, 2010.

ADDITIONAL CGN RESOURCES

CO✝RAGEOUS
GRANDPARENTING
SEMINARS & CONFERENCES

Courageous Grandparenting Conferences and Seminars designed to challenge today's Christian grandparents to courageously embrace their biblical roles so that their grandchildren may know, love and serve Christ. Host a conference or seminar in your church or community. Information about hosting a seminar or an upcoming conference can be found at the CGN website.

Join with thousands of grandparents across this land each year on the Sunday following Labor Day as we make National Grandparents Day at day of prayer and fasting for our grandchildren, their parents and our nation. Visit our web site at *www.christiangrandparenting.net/day-of-prayer* to find out how you can organize a prayer event in your church or community.

Grandparents at Prayer

G@P groups meet regularly throughout the year to prayer for each other's grandchildren and families. Join a group or organize one in your area. Click on the G@P icon on our web site to find out more.

Since 1998 the Christian Grandparenting Network has produced GrandCamps each summer for grandparents and their grade-school age grandchildren. Now, GrandCamps is going national as a strategic program offering to various camps, churches and denominations. A complete GrandCamp curriculum will be available, along with all resources needed to host this program in your own church or camp/conference facility, beginning November 2013. *A Do-It-Yourself* version will also be available by Spring 2014 for grandparents who would like ideas and resources for doing their own GrandCamp or Cousins' Camp. Visit www.grandcamps.org for details.

GOSPELSHAPEDFAMILY
EQUIPPING FAMILIES FOR GOSPEL SHAPED LIVING

Gospel Shaped Family (GSF) provides a unique conference experience for both parents and grandparents. This two-day family conference is designed to equip families to raise children and grandchildren with a deep, lasting, culture-transforming faith. God designed families to shape the next generation with the gospel, give them a biblical view of life, and be the primary means to help children and grandchildren mature in Christ.

There is no other conference like the Gospel Shaped Family Conference.

My Hope for You offers a powerful online tool to help grandparents write their story for another generation. MH2Y helps you tell your faith story and produce it in a beautiful full-color printed book with your own photos you choose. Find out more at www.myhopeforyou.org.

4Gens provides a pure discipleship model for families. Using a one-on-one approach combined with online tools, 4Gens trains and nurtures parents and grandparents to pass on to another generation what they've learned and know to be true. www.4gens.com

Christian Grandparenting Network
www.christiangrandparenting.net
5844 Pioneer Mesa Dr.
Colorado Springs, CO 80923
719-522-1404